Elaine Ku

HEALING
with

SPIRIT

HEALTH INTUITION, CLAIRVOYANCE, AND AFTERLIFE COMMUNICATION

REDFeather

MIND | BODY | SPIRIT

Other Schiffer Books by Elaine Kuzmeskus

The Art of Mediumship: Psychic Investigation, Clairvoyance, and Channeling
ISBN: 978-0-7643-4016-1

Séance 101: Physical Links to the Other Side
ISBN: 978-0-7643-2717-9

Connecticut Ghosts: Spirits in the State of Steady Habits
ISBN: 978-0-7643-2361-4

Type set in Desire/ Adobe Caslon
ISBN: 978-0-7643-5638-4
Printed in China

Published by Red Feather Mind, Body, Spirit
An imprint of Schiffer Publishing, Ltd.
4880 Lower Valley Road
Atglen, PA 19310
Phone: (610) 593-1777; Fax: (610) 593-2002
E-mail: Info@schifferbooks.com
Web: www.schifferbooks.com

For our complete selection of fine books on this and related subjects, please visit our website at www.schifferbooks.com. You may also write for a free catalog.

Schiffer Publishing's titles are available at special discounts for bulk purchases for sales promotions or premiums. Special editions, including personalized covers, corporate imprints, and excerpts, can be created in large quantities for special needs. For more information, contact the publisher.

We are always looking for people to write books on new and related subjects. If you have an idea for a book, please contact us at proposals@schifferbooks.com.

Disclaimer: The author is not a doctor not does she dispense medical advice or prescribe the use of any technique as a form of diagnosis or treatment for any physical, emotional, or medical condition. The reader should consult his or her medical, health, or other professional before adopting any of the suggestions in this book.

Healing with Spirit is dedicated to all my students
of metaphysical healing—Reiki, hypnosis, and medical mediumship.
As you heal with your hands and heart, thoughts, and spirit,
remember the words from *The Prophet:* "Work is love made visible."

Acknowledgments

I have been blessed by many excellent teachers. First and foremost, Spiritualist minsters, Rev. Gladys Custance and Rev. Kenneth Custance, who taught me hands on healing and the power of prayer. I would also like acknowledge Reiki Master William Rand, who trained me in Reiki I, II, and master level, along with Carlos Gonzales and his wife, Ana, for Karuna Reiki training. Next, I wish to thank mediums Rev. Alex Orbito and John of God for showing the full potential of spiritual healing. Many thanks also go to the Theosophical Society of America, as well as the Association for Research and Enlightenment for their assistance. Finally, I would like to acknowledge Susan Roberts for fine editing skills and insightful comments. She, along with Dinah Roseberry and the staff of Schiffer Publishing have given *Healing with Spirit* its final polish.

Contents

Healing with Spirit

Author with Rev. Alex Orbito.
Courtesy Ronald J. Kuzmeskus.

"There are two things of which I am certain," I told my parapsychology students in 1993. "One, the psychic surgery on the video is genuine, and two, I have no idea how Alex Orbito does it." I could give them no simple explanation for the phenomenon that we had just witnessed on a VHS video. The healer had literally plunged his hand into the patient's body to remove black, diseased tissue.

The Introduction to Parapsychology class at Asnuntuck Community College was typical for Connecticut students in the early 1990s. Several men and woman worked for Hartford insurance companies, others were housewives, a few were regular college students who were researching the paranormal, and two or three were retirees. Nothing in their lives prepared them for such unorthodox mediumship. Even though Alex Orbito had recently been featured in Shirley MacLaine's book *Going Within*, the healer was relatively unknown in the United States.

After watching the video, I became fascinated by psychic healing. When I heard the healer from the Philippines was coming to Lancaster, Pennsylvania, I knew I had to see for myself how he accomplished psychic surgery. Since my husband, Ronald, had been out of work with a back injury, I thought it would be a good idea if Ron went for a healing as well. After a five-hour drive from Connecticut, my husband and I arrived at a suburban Pennsylvania farm house. We were told to unbuckle our slacks and open our shirts, since the surgery would be brief without much time to adjust clothing. Then about forty people age twenty to seventy—many of whom were nurses, chiropractors, and mediums—lined up for treatment. Everyone was enthusiastic but a bit nervous.

When my turn came, I went to an upstairs bedroom that had been turned into a clinic. Alex and his assistant, a woman dressed in white, helped me onto a massage table. As I lay on the table with my shirt pulled up, I felt excited but vulnerable. Just before I closed my eyes to recite "The Lord's Prayer," I looked into Alex's compassionate brown eyes. By the time I silently recited "I shall not want," I felt pressure on my chest. The psychic surgeon's fingers entered my chest cavity, and I could actually feel his fingers massaging my heart.

Was the process painful? No, but I definitely felt pressure, and a few drops of blood spurted out. The three-minute "surgery" left me light-headed. My chest had red marks, which faded within twenty-four hours. No stitches were required.

The real miracle that weekend was the healing Ron received. He had been unable to work for the past three years due to his back injury. As Ron put it, his upper neck killed him, and he felt as if there was an ice pick in his back, right between the shoulder blades. After four psychic surgeries that weekend, the cervical pain in his upper back was completely gone, and the spirit doctors lowered the "ice pick" to the base of his spine. While he could still feel some pain in his back, it was transformed to a dull ache in the lower region. In fact, Ron felt so good that he went back to work as a master sprinkler fitter.

Since then, we have traveled to Brazil and England and across the United States and Canada to learn more about healing with spirit. In addition to Reverend Alex Orbito, there are many fine mediums who heal. For instance, John of God has healed hundreds of thousands in Brazil and all over the world. In England, Steve Upton, under the guidance of the spirit of Dr. Liston, has given scores of healings. Upton works in the tradition of British Spiritualist Harry Edwards.

In the United States, energy medicine is becoming popular through the work of Donna Eden and Caroline Myss. Many doctors, including Richard Gerber, author of *Vibrational Medicine*, and Dr. Norman Shealy, author of *Medical Intuition*, recommend the use of spiritual healing. The doctor who coined the term "medical intuitive" believes that many of our current illnesses have their roots in our past lives. After almost twenty-five years of investigating healing mediums, I tell my students at the New England School of Metaphysics, "I know that healing with spirit is real, and I can explain how it works."

CHAPTER ONE

Holy Medicine

Those who overcome others are powerful.
Those who overcome themselves are strong.
Those who know others are wise.
Those who know themselves are enlightened.

—Lao Tzu

Ever since the building of the pyramids, people have sought help from the spirit side of life. For thousands of years, spiritual healing has been honored not only in ancient Egypt, but also in Greece, India, and China, and later in the West. This knowledge of the ancient world can be found in the pyramids of Giza and the mysterious Sphinx, as well as the Greek temples and the sacred texts of India channeled by rishis.

Egyptians were the first to document the spirit world in *The Egyptian Book of the Dead.* They believed that the spirit left the body at death—and also in dreams and in states of deep relaxation or trance. This book furthermore wards off the presence of evil spirits in the afterlife and tells the deceased how to avoid them. It describes judgment in the Hall of Records, where souls are judged for their good and foolish deeds.

Ancient Egyptians also practiced spiritual healing, since they believed that illnesses were caused by unhappy spirits. Egyptian patients accepted the psychic cures as readily as modern man accepts psychology. Magic, incantations, and amulets were employed to rid the ill of negative spirits and prevent their return. The ancient Egyptians were also known to invoke the power of their gods and goddesses to drive out unwanted influences. Chief among the Egyptian deities were Osiris, god in charge of the afterlife; his son, Horus, a sky god; Thoth; a moon deity; and Ra, the sun god. Female deities included Isis known for magic and Hathor, goddess of love. The Egyptians also honored Amon, creator god and Ptah, patron of craftsmen. Anubis was the god of mummification. At death, this jackal-headed god weighed the heart against the feather of truth. The Ibis-headed god, Thoth, stood by to record the results. Should the heart equal the weight of the feather, then the deceased was allowed into the afterlife; otherwise, he or she would be devoured by Ammit, composed of the deadly crocodile, lion, and hippopotamus.

Above all, the Egyptians prayed to the goddess of healing, Sekhmet. She is portrayed as a lioness, and she is so powerful that her breath formed the desert. This goddess led the Egyptians into warfare, and was chosen as the protector of the pharaohs.[1] Frequently, amulets would have a picture of Sekhmet or another god to ward off evil spirits. Sometimes the amulets bore inscriptions for protection from a specific god.

Egyptologist Sir Ernest Wallis Budge described the ancient civilization as having "a lofty spiritual character," in which prophecy, mediumship, and healing played a central role. They used incense, chanting, magical incantations, crystals, and clairvoyance, as well as herbs and amulets fashioned form malachite, lapis lazuli, turquoise, tiger's eye, and amethysts. These stones were valued as much for their precious nature as for their magic. Incantations were said or ingredients were rubbed over the amulet to grant the owner's particular wish.[2]

While the Egyptians petitioned many gods, the ancient Greeks focused on one, Asclepius, who they believed was the god in charge of healing. The Greeks built hundreds of temples dedicated to Asclepius. In ca. 430 BC, the most famous temple dedicated to Asclepius was near the east coast of southern Greece, at Epidaurus. In many ways, these temples functioned as hospitals, taking in seriously ill patients and providing them with sanctuary. Roman emperor Antoninus Pius added a 180-room structure for the dying and for women in childbirth. Temples such as that of Epidaurus were built in wooded valleys where they were close to springs and caves,

Ancient Egyptian hieroglyph that shows the heart being weighed
on the scale of Maat against the feather of truth by the jackal-headed god, Anubis.
Egyptian Book of the Dead.

which the Greeks believed to be places where "good spirits" dwelled. Here, the priest practiced a process of healing known as *incubation*. While the patient was asleep in the temple, he or she would be visited by Asclepius in a dream. In the morning the priest would arrive to interpret the dreams and prescribe treatment.[3]

The Greeks' philosophical life also differed from that of the Egyptians. For instance, Pythagoreans wanted to understand the revelations of the Mysteries and not wait for death to release them from the burdens of the body. Plato inherited much from Pythagoras, as well as his mentor Socrates, who was known for his intelligence, intellectual honesty, and disdain for public acclaim. Even Socrates believed in spirit guides. "The favor of the gods," said Socrates, "has given me a marvelous gift, which has never left me since my childhood. It is a voice which, when it makes itself heard, deters me from what I am about to do and never urges me on."[4]

The voice of spirit was also heard by Apollonius of Tyana, who was familiar with the practice the Hermetic principles. "They are intermediate powers of a divine order. They fashion dreams, inspire soothsayers," says Apuleius. "They are inferior immortals, called gods of the second rank, placed between earth and heaven," notes Maximus of Tyre. Plato thinks that a kind of spirit, which is separate from us, receives man at his birth and follows him in life and after death. He calls it "the daimon which has received us as its portion." The ancient idea of the daimon seems, therefore, to be analogous to the guardian angel of Christians.

When Socrates was executed by the state on the charge of corrupting Athenian youth, his last words were "We ought to offer a cock to Asclepius." Thus, Socrates acknowledged his belief in life after death, since sacrificing a cock to Asclepius was traditionally as a way of giving thanks to the god of healing for recovering from an illness. For Socrates, life in this corrupt world was as an illness; death provided a return to a timeless world.

The most famous of the physicians trained in the Asclepius method of healing was Hippocrates, the "Father of Medicine." He believed that diseases were not a punishment of the gods but rather due to environmental causes. Hippocrates is best known for the Hippocratic Oath, taken by all physicians. The original oath was written in the late fifth century and requires a new doctor to swear, by a number of healing gods, to uphold specific ethical standards.[5] When taking the Hippocratic Oath, today's physicians are no longer required to pledge their allegiance to the gods, but they promise *"primum non nocere"*: first do not harm.

After Hippocrates, the next important physician was Claudius Galenus, or Galen, a Greek who lived from AD 129 to 200. Romans flocked to Greek doctors such as Galen, who also thought that the soul contributed to the overall health of the body. He favored a holistic approach because he believed there to be no distinction between the mental and the physical. Galen also believed that the soul contributed to the overall health of the body. One of Galen's major works, *On the Diagnosis and*

Cure of the Soul's Passion, was an early attempt at psychotherapy, since it prompted individuals to reveal their deepest passions and secrets in order to cure their mental maladies. The therapist was usually an older, wiser male, in control of his emotions

Other ancient cultures that believed in healing with spirit entities include India and China. Even today, many Hindus believe in astrology, as well as the Vedas, which were channeled by rishis some 5,000 years ago. According to Dr. Andrew Weil, "Ayurveda medicine is a system that originated in northern India over 5,000 years ago. It is primarily from one of the Vedic texts, the ancient books of wisdom and ceremony that contributed a great deal to the foundation of Indian culture and civilization. It includes a system of herbalism, but also offers dietary regulation, yoga, and other exercises, bodywork, detoxification, and psychological interventions."[6]

In China, spirit mediums known as "wu" practiced healing as well as divination well over 3,000 years ago. The practice of communicating with the dead through a medium was widely accepted, since the Chinese believed that the wu could call souls down from the dead: Wang Ch'ung chronicled channeling called wu, a practice commonly accepted in China in the first century AD. "Among men, the dead speak through living persons whom they throw into a trance, and the wu, thrumming black chords, call down the souls of the dead who speak through the mouth of the wu."[7]

Much of China's Taoist literature and Tibetan philosophy are believed to have come through channeled sources, as well as the work of its philosophers. The most honored of the philosophers was the Buddha, who came to teach the path of enlightenment, which includes the concept of reincarnation. He was born in Nepal in 563 BC. After living a life as Prince Gautama, Buddha achieved enlightenment while meditating under a bodi tree during the full moon in May. His teachings spread his knowledge throughout Asia, establishing many schools, with the most mystic branch found in Tibet.

One of the most revered of the Tibetan mystics is Milarepa (1052–1135). In the beginning, Milarepa was seduced by sorcery, which displeased his guru. To teach his disciple a lesson, the guru had him build and rebuild a house several times. Eventually, Milarepa realized the misuse of his mystic powers through magic. He turned away from the world and became a hermit. In seclusion, he developed the powers of levitation and astral travel. He also was known for his excellent voice, and he composed many hymns that are still sung in Tibet today.[8]

While Eastern civilizations had a rich tradition of spiritual knowledge, the West also had its interest in mysticism. Western civilization stems from three cultures: the Judeo-Christian, the Greek, and the Roman. The Bible is the basis for our current code of morality. From the Greeks, we received knowledge concerning art, education, philosophy, medicine, and science. In fact, much of our nation's laws and systems of government stem from the Romans.

Each of these civilizations held its prophets in high esteem. The Bible refers to Old Testament prophets Abraham, Jeremiah, and Ezekiel with respect. In the New

Testament, the birth of Christ is foretold by astrologers, "the three wise men." Jesus became famous throughout the country for his healing. Many thought of him as a healing rabbi: "And Jesus went about all Galilee, teaching in their synagogues, preaching the gospel of the kingdom, and healing all kinds of sickness and all kinds of disease among the people. Then His fame went throughout all Syria, and they brought to Him all sick people who were afflicted with various diseases and torments, and those who were demon-possessed, epileptics, and paralytics; and He healed them."[9]

The early Christians by necessity were a secret society. They were viciously persecuted by the power-hungry Romans until AD 306, when Constantine became emperor. Some, such as the Gnostics, were able to preserve their records written on scrolls in caves in the town of Nag Hammadi. These records, known as the Dead Sea Scrolls, were discovered in 1947 and emphasized the Gnostics' belief in knowledge over blind faith. The Dead Sea Scrolls were written by the Essenes, a group that is mentioned by the historian Josephus. "The Essenes were a strict Torah observant, Messianic, and apocalyptic, baptist, wilderness, new covenant Jewish sect. They were led by a priest they called the 'Teacher of Righteousness,' who was opposed and possibly killed by the establishment priesthood in Jerusalem."[10]

After the persecution of the Christians, society plunged into the Dark Ages. However, monks continued to copy the Bible and keep the spiritual presence of Christ alive. Chief among them was Saint Francis of Assisi. Saint Francis shunned materialism and would allow his monks to possess only the clothes on their backs. He was credited with many healings and is remembered for his great kindness to man and beast alike. He healed the lame and blind. His miracles also included restoring life to those who had been pronounced dead. For example, a mother from the Pomarico area had a vision of Saint Francis following the sudden death of her little daughter: "The saint appeared to assure the fate of his beloved daughter. Shortly after, the little girl awoke to the wonder of those present, and stood up as if nothing had happened."[11]

During the Middle Ages, some enlightened healers such as Paracelsus turned to alchemy, astrology, and natural remedies. The doctor even treated syphilis, gout, leprosy, and ulcers with mercury. Paracelsus, moreover, is believed to have discovered mesmerism or hypnosis: "He believed the Hermetic principle that human beings had a vital body (an etheric double created and energized by the vital force of the universe) and that when this vital body was depleted, physical ailment was the result."[12] He also thought that the vital body could be reenergized by contact with a healer who had an abundance of the life force. Anton Mesmer later was credited with the discovery of magnetic healing; however, Paracelsus was well aware of what Mesmer termed "animal magnetism."

In the 1700s, one man, Emanuel Swedenborg (1688–1772), emerged to open the spiritual eyes of the public. His own clairvoyance began at age fifty-three. The scientist-turned-seer wrote eighteen books on the afterlife, including *Heaven and Hell*, which was published in 1758. He believed that the afterlife mirrored that on earth: "Life in Spirit is similar to that on the Earth plane, with houses, churches, schools, etc. The process of death is said by Angels (good spirits) that everyone rests for a few days after death and then regains full consciousness."[13] As people adjust to the Other Side, they regain their vigor and are allowed to progress to higher levels.

Swedenborg's writings are similar in vein to those of Andrew Jackson Davis (1826–1910). Davis received messages from spirit in much the same manner as ancient Greek oracles received information from the god Apollo. His guides included the spirit of the Greek physician Marcus Galen and the spirit of Swedish seer Emmanuel Swedenborg. One particularly vivid vision, which occurred on the evening of March 6, 1844, changed the course of Davis's life. Davis experienced what Spiritualists term "traveling clairvoyance," which is similar to what is termed "remote viewing" today.

In this out-of-body state, Andrew Jackson Davis traveled clairvoyantly to mountains some forty miles away. Here, he made contact with the spirits of Marcus Galen and Emanuel Swedenborg. The Roman physician told the young medium about the healing power of nature and provided him with a magic staff with strips with cures for diseases with the message "Under all circumstances, keep an even mind."[14]

Andrew Jackson Davis's first series of trance lectures resulted in a 700-page book, *The Principles of Nature, Her Divine Revelations, and a Voice to Mankind*. In its pages, spirit explained to readers that "The Divine Mind is the Cause, the Universe is the Effect, and Spirit is the ultimate Design."[15] He soon became known for his prophecy as well as healing ability. For instance, he predicted the existence of the planets Neptune and Pluto many years before their actual discovery.[16]

Shortly after the birth of Spiritualism and Spiritism at the turn of the century, Edgar Cayce, the "Sleeping Prophet," began his work. Edgar Cayce was the most documented "medical intuitive" in the twentieth century. He gave over 9,000 medical/health readings during a forty-year period. With virtually no medical training—not even a high school diploma—while in a deep trance, he helped thousands of people over the years. He provided them with insight into their physical, mental, and spiritual health, as well as recommending alternative cures such a castor oil packs, massage, and natural remedies.

Cayce's guide, known as the Source, continually advised that the current life is only a stage in our evolution. According to Cayce, "Death—as commonly spoken of—is only the passing through God's other door."[17] His guide, the Source, further explained that people maintain their personalities in the change called death: Do not consider for a moment that an individual soul-entity passing from earth plane as a Catholic, a Methodist, or an Episcopalian is something else because he is dead! He is only a dead Episcopalian, Catholic, or Methodist."

CHAPTER TWO

Esoteric Anatomy

I swear by Apollo Physician and Asclepius and Hygeia and Panacea and all the gods and goddesses, making them my witnesses, that I will fulfill according to my ability and judgment this oath and this covenant.

—Hippocratic Oath, classical version[1]

The ancient Greeks believed in body, mind, and spirit. When the ancient physicians took their oaths, they pledged allegiance to "Apollo Physician and Asclepius and Hygeia and Panacea and all the gods and goddesses." A modern-day doctor would be aghast at such an oath. However, to the ancients, the spirit world was a reality.

Psychologist Elizabeth Mayer turned to this hidden world as a last resort. When her eleven-year-old daughter's harp was stolen, she contacted a dowser, Harold McCoy, in Fayetteville, Arkansas. The president of the American Society for Dowsers requested a street map of her Oakland, California, neighborhood and two days later called to tell her the exact location of her daughter's prized harp. "Well, I got that harp located," he said. "It's in the second house on the right on D—— Street, just off L—— Avenue."[2] After cleverly placing a poster offering a reward for the safe return of the harp nearby the address, she was able to negotiate its return.

Apparently, there are hidden energies that dowsers can access. The ancient Chinese called the spirit energy "chi"; the Japanese, "ki"; and in the martial arts, it is called "qi." The Hindus referred to the invisible force that surrounds the body as "prana." This energy is also known as "the diamond body" in Taoism, "the light body" or "rainbow body" in Tibetan Buddhism, and "the body of bliss" in Kriya yoga.

In the nineteenth century, this force was termed the "astral light" by theosophists, "animal magnetism" by Doctor Franz Anton Mesmer, and "odic force" by Baron Karl von Reichenbach. He dubbed the energy "odic" after the Norse god Odin and explained its function in a long article, "Researches on Magnetism, Electricity, Heat, and Light in their Relations to Vital Forces." He believed that the odic force had both a positive and negative charge that emanated from the body, particularly from the hands, mouth, and forehead.[3] Eventually, Reichenbach hoped to develop scientific proof for a universal life force; however, his experiments relied on perceptions

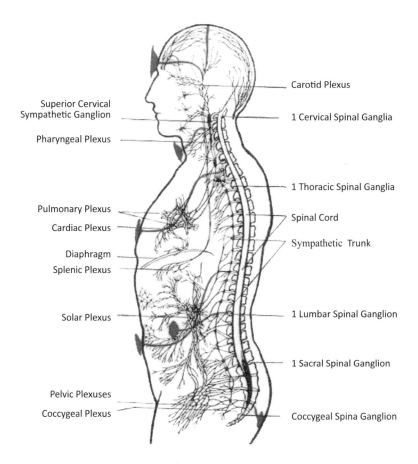

Superior Cervical Sympathetic Ganglion

Pharyngeal Plexus

Pulmonary Plexus

Cardiac Plexus

Diaphragm

Splenic Plexus

Solar Plexus

Pelvic Plexuses

Coccygeal Plexus

Carotid Plexus

1 Cervical Spinal Ganglia

1 Thoracic Spinal Ganglia

Spinal Cord

Sympathetic Trunk

1 Lumbar Spinal Ganglion

1 Sacral Spinal Ganglion

Coccygeal Spina Ganglion

THE CHAKRAS AND THE NERVOUS SYSTEM

Diagram from *The Chakras*, by C. W. Leadbeater.
Courtesy of the Theosophical Society of America.

reported by individuals who claimed to be "sensitive," since he himself could not observe any of the reported phenomena. The "sensitives" had to work in total or near-total darkness to be able to observe the phenomena. He felt that with training, about a third of the population could see the odic force around people.[3]

What the baron called odic energy was described as "chi" over 2,000 years ago in the Chinese classic *The Yellow Emperor's Classic of Internal Medicine*. Another classic Chinese text dating back to ca. 1668–1692, *The Secret of the Golden Flower*, was first translated into German by Richard Wilhelm. His friend Carl Jung provided a commentary to the book on Taoism and alchemy. The book gives information on meditation techniques, as well as procedures for posture, control of the breath, and contemplation: "Sitting primarily relates to a straight posture. Breathing is described in detail, primarily in terms of the esoteric physiology of the path of *qi* (also known as *chi* or *ki*), or breath energy. The energy path associated with breathing has been described as similar to an internal wheel vertically aligned with the spine. When breathing is steady, the wheel turns forward, with breath energy rising in back and descending in front. Bad breathing habits (or bad posture, or even bad thoughts) may cause the wheel not to turn, or move backward, inhibiting the circulation of essential breath energy. In contemplation, one watches thoughts as they arise and recede."[4]

One of the first Western scientists to investigate the human energy field was Dr. Walter Kilner. He even invented a device to see the aura by using a glass lens covered by a blue dye. In 1911, Dr. Kilner published his findings in the book *The Human Atmosphere*. Kilner explained that he was able to perceive auric formations, which he termed the Etheric Double, the Inner Aura, and the Outer Aura.

Sir Oliver Lodge and theosophist Arthur E. Powell were intrigued by Kilner's research. Powell incorporated Kilner's findings in his book, *The Etheric Double*. While he was enthusiastic about Kilner's work, Powell made it clear that Kilner had a view different than that of theosophists. Unlike Dr. Kilner, who wished to use knowledge for medical purposes, Powell focused on spiritual studies. He believed that the astral body was primitive for those of lower mentality, but it became a means of awakening to higher planes for those who were mentally alert.

Powell also believed that "one of the first things a man learns to do in his astral body is to travel in it—it being possible for the astral body to move with great rapidity and to great distances from the sleeping physical body. An understanding of this phenomenon throws much light on a large number of so-called 'occult' phenomena, such as 'apparitions' of many kinds, knowledge of places never visited physically, etc."[5]

Theosophist Charles Webster Leadbeater conducted an extensive study of the chakras, outlined in *The Chakras*. The book, first published in 1927, contains a number of vividly colored diagrams of the energy center that serve as psychic sense organs. Leadbeater also used his clairvoyant powers to observe the seven bodies, each with a particular function.. He also noted that there were seven locations that are used to receive and distribute astral energies throughout the human system. Each of these seven centers, or chakras, is connected to the physical body via the endocrine system of ductless glands. These glands secrete hormones as well as electromagnetically charged fluids directly into the blood and nervous system.

Leadbeater's clairvoyance was so remarkable that he was able to peer inside an atom before microscopes were invented that were powerful enough to penetrate the atom's microscopic structure. When microscopes did view the atom, scientists saw the same structures Leadbeater had described many years before in *Occult Chemistry*, which he coauthored with Annie Besant. "The book consists both of coordinated and illustrated descriptions of presumed etheric counterparts of the atoms of the then known chemical elements, and of other expositions of occult physics."[6]

The chakras also serve a spiritual purpose. According to Vedic literature, every individual has seven bodies—physical, etheric, astral, lower mental, higher mental, spiritual, and Cosmic Consciousness. As a person meditates and lives a spiritual life, the kundalini power at the base of the spine travels up the spine. When the kundalini is raised through the center or chakras of the body, an ordinary person experiences creativity, intuition, and even cosmic consciousness.

Seven Bodies

Physical body	Three-dimensional body
Etheric double	Exact duplicate of the physical body, made of finer material
Astral body	Finer-energy body used during the sleep state for astral travel
Mental body	Lower mental body associated with intellect and rational thought
Manas	Higher mental body associated with spirituality and intuitive thought
Buddhic body	Individual portion of God, associated with "third eye"
God or Atma	God or Cosmic consciousness

The etheric body contains seven vital organs or chakras, with 72,000 nadis to carry the life force or prana throughout the body. Leadbeater, in his book *Chakras*, described their color, function, and position in the body. Each chakra has spokes of energy radiating from the center. As the chakras go up the spine, they increase in the number of spokes, radiation, and intensity. For example, the first chakra or root chakra has four spokes, while the crown chakra is known as "the lotus of a thousand petals." The centers also range in color from infrared to ultraviolet. Each chakra has a psychological function as well.

The **first chakra**, of four petals, is located at the base of the spine. It keeps the individual grounded. When this chakra is out of balance—often signaled by lower back pain—the person has security issues. Its color is red, and it is associated with the flight-or-fight response to stress.

The **second chakra**, of six petals, is located over the spleen and rules the sex glands. People with a strong second chakra exude warmth. When this second chakra is deregulated, sexual indulgence and a desire for glamour and attention can manifest. In the East, worldly success is seen as a detriment to spiritual progress.

The **third chakra**, which contains ten petals, is located in the area of the solar plexus. People with a strong third chakra have a well-developed intellect, leadership skills, and confidence. When there is dysfunction, fear and subsequent indecision will reign. Often these indecisive people suffer from stomach problems, especially ulcers.

The **fourth chakra** is located in the center of the chest at the heart level. It has twelve petals and is associated with the color green. It governs the thymus gland and rules compassion. When this center is depressed, disorders of the heart and immune system may suffer.

The **fifth chakra**, located in the throat area, has sixteen petals and rules the thyroid. Its color is turquoise blue. When opened, it allows for creativity and clarity of mind. Imbalances in this chakra can cause speech and throat problems.

The last three chakras have psychic potentials: the fifth, clairaudience; the sixth, clairvoyance; the seventh, Cosmic Consciousness.

The **sixth chakra**, indigo blue in color, has ninety-six petals and is associated with the pineal gland. When it is opened, faith, spiritual vision, and even clairvoyance may manifest. However, when it is deregulated, depression, eye problems, and headaches may manifest.

The **seventh chakra**, called the crown chakra, has 960 petals and rules the master gland of the body, the pituitary gland. Known in the East as "the lotus of a thousand petals," it is a center for Cosmic Consciousness. However, a soul may experience dysfunction and remain trapped emotionally between the two worlds, such as in a physical coma or a psychological condition called schizophrenia, which affects one percent of the population. When this chakra is opened in a positive manner, the aspirant attains self liberation and freedom from rebirth.

In sleep, the physical body with its etheric double remains on the bed, while the astral body is free to leave. According to C. W. Leadbeater, "Clairvoyant observation bears abundant testimony to the fact that when a man falls into a deep slumber, the higher principles in their astral vehicle almost invariably withdraw from the body and hover in its immediate neighborhood. Indeed, it is the process of this withdrawal that we commonly call 'going to sleep.'"[7] Often the astral body is directed by desire. "This astral vehicle is even more sensitive to external impressions than the gross and etheric bodies, for it is itself the seat of all desires and emotions—the connecting link through which alone the ego can collect experiences from physical life. It is peculiarly susceptible to the influence of passing thought-currents, and when the mind is not actively controlling it, it is perpetually receiving these stimuli from without, and eagerly responding to them."[8] For instance, a mother concerned about an adult child may travel to where he or she is residing to visit. A spiritual aspirant, on the other hand, may go to halls of higher learning on the Other Side.

Channeler Edgar Cayce agreed with much of C. W. Leadbeater's information on the chakras. According to the "Sleeping Prophet," meditation, prayers, and service to others are the best way to achieve a spiritual life. He truly believed "the psychic is of the soul."

Since Edgar Cayce's day, physicians such as Dr. Douglas Baker have studied esoteric anatomy. Baker studied the work of Alice Bailey, who channeled a Tibetan Master. Dr. Baker also openly discussed his spirit guide, the Master Robert Browning. From his esoteric studies, Baker came to the conclusion that "ninety percent of the cause of man's disease lie in planes other than the physical, and it is on those planes that symptoms manifest first before they work through to manifest as gross physical disorders."[9]

According to Dr. Baker, we feel in our astral body and think in our mental body. During sleep, we leave our physical-etheric body on the bed and move about the astral and mental planes in our astral-mental body. "But in deep coma, such as produced by alcohol in any quantity, the astral body cannot leave the physical, cannot in fact come out of alignment with it. It is anchored to the physical body because of the massive metabolic activity going on in the liver and because of the excessive stimulation of the Solar Plexus Chakra resulting from it."[10] Thus, the lack of natural sleep can lead to depression and lower immune system and liver issues. In its later stages, the alcoholic may become stuck on the lower astral plane and experience delirium tremens.

Dr. Baker also views disease as a form of spiritual purification: "Disease is a purifying process . . . the healer helps the patient to endure whilst the disease purifies. Disease is the way in which the soul adjusts its personality vehicles so that they can remain in contact with the environment or, through disease, the soul is able to terminate its need for expression in that particular life, or finally, through disease the soul may deliberately end a personality situation, which offers to it nothing but the opposite of its intent."[11]

Rev. Rosalyn Bruyere, author of *Wheels of Light*, also uses her clairvoyant abilities to view the link between the body, mind, and the soul. For example, she advised Dr.

Jonathan Kramer, a patient who had a cancerous tumor. "This is pretty big stuff when your body tells you that your job is killing you in a very specific way," says Bruyere. "You're pretty much going to have to deal with all your core assumptions."[12] Fortunately, he followed her advice and survived with a more positive view of life. Rev. Bruyere has helped many other celebrity clients, including Cher, Barbra Streisand, James Coburn, and director Frank Zappa.

She has been an inspiration to many healers, including Barbara Ann Brennan, author of *Hands of Light*. In 1987, she established the Barbara Ann Brennan School of Healing. According to Brennan, the auric field is the vehicle for all psychosomatic reactions: "The auric field is a quantum leap deeper into our personality than is our physical body. It is at this level of our being that our psychological processes take place. The Human Energy Field is the vehicle for all psychosomatic reactions."[13]

Another medical intuitive, Caroline Myss, collaborated with physician Dr. Norman Shealy. Later, in 1996, Myss authored *Anatomy of Spirit*, a book that combines the seven Christian sacraments with the seven Hindu chakras. Currently, Myss heads Caroline Myss Educational Institute, which she founded in 2003. Caroline Myss, Rosalyn Bruyere, and Barbara Ann Brennan all agree that each of us has the potential to transform through the chakra system. As Paramahansa Yogananda said many years before, "When an ordinary man puts the necessary time and enthusiasm in meditation and prayer, he becomes a divine man."

Affirmations

Energy follows thought. One way to heal yourself is to change your thinking. When you feel worried, try using self-hypnosis in the form of a positive thought, such as an affirmation. Since it is impossible to hold two thoughts in your mind at the same time, focusing on an affirmation will overcome tension and worry, which are barriers to healing.

Elwood Babbitt, a premier channeler, gave this affirmation for health: "I have a God-sound mind in a God-sound body." One of Reverend Gladys Custance's favorite affirmations was "A mighty God force goes before me making easy, instant, and perfect my way." When late for an appointment, try this: "Divine order prevails in my life." To improve your psychic ability, say or think "I am keen, vital, and alert in the activity of spirit."

The key to using affirmations is sincere desire to improve the situation.

Peace Meditation

When anger or depression enters the thought field, common sense and compassion are quickly negated. People will naturally shut down. On a psychological level, anger is directed outward, while depression is anger turned inward. On an esoteric level, angry emotions are an irritant to the soul, while depressed thoughts siphon its life force. Either way, the ego and its corresponding third chakra suffer. Young people are particularly sensitive and may be influenced by the negative emotions of others, as well as their own impulsive thoughts. It is possible, however, to shift the negative energy by placing it in a higher chakra with guided imagery.

For instance, when strong emotions of depression block your heart center, try this exercise, which was given to me in my twenties during a period of transition. Dr. Douglas Baker suggested that I shift the energy from my solar plexus or third chakra to the heart center, which is in the middle of the chest at heart level. The heart chakra is a balance point in the aura and rules the rational mind. Try this calming exercise when life's troubles overwhelm you. It is particularly helpful to those who feel that they are in danger of becoming an emotional door mat for the negativity of those around them.

> Sit or lie down in a comfortable position. Be sure to turn the phone off and pull the shades down so you are in a quiet and darkened environment. Have a friend read this script slowly to you. If you prefer, you can read the script into a tape recorder and play it back.
>
> Take a moment to still your body.
>
> Breathe in peace. Exhale all negative emotions.
>
> Repeat this process three times.
>
> Visualize yourself surrounded by white light.
>
> Now, place your dominant hand about six inches from your solar plexus or stomach.
>
> Wait thirty seconds or more until you feel your hand drawing energy.
>
> Bring this energy from your solar plexus to your heart center in the middle of your chest.
>
> Repeat several times, until you feel a shift in energy from excessive emotion to peace of mind.
>
> As you do each sweep slowly, you may wish to add a positive affirmation, such as "Divine mind prevails, "I have a God-sound mind in a God-sound body," or "Divine harmony prevails."

CHAPTER THREE

Developing Intuition

*The intuitive mind is a sacred gift
and the rational mind is a faithful servant. We have created a
society that honors the servant and has forgotten the gift.*

—Dr. Albert Einstein

Dr. Carl Jung. *Public domain.*

A sign in Albert Einstein's office is said to have read, "Not everything that can be counted counts, and not everything that counts can be counted." The famous physicist was ahead of his time. So was psychologist Dr. Carl Jung, who believed in four types of thought: direct sensation, emotion, intellect, and intuition. Everyone has intuitive thought to some degree of another. Some people call it mother's intuition; others, gut feeling; and many, just a hunch.

If anyone should know a thing or two about intuition, it is Joe McMoneagle, the author of *Remote Viewing Secrets*. His quest to understand intuition began as a soldier in the US Army: "My life was saved more than once by simply doing what my inner voices suggested, even if at the time it seemed foolish or stupid, or that I might embarrass myself."[1] Following his intuition kept McMoneagle safe in the jungles of Vietnam.

It also guided him through a near-death experience in Germany that occurred when someone secretly slipped a toxic substance into his predinner cocktail. Before he knew it, he was out of his body, looking down at someone frantically trying to revive him when he went into convulsions and swallowed his tongue. After his recovery in a German hospital, he began to have a series of psychic experiences in which he could read the minds of those around him: "I wasn't actually hearing them thinking, nor was I reading their thoughts verbatim, but I was picking up on the general gist or subject matter contained within their thoughts. It was almost like seeing through an upper layer to another layer underneath."[2] Soon he was reading books on Eastern philosophy and perusing the writing of Helena Blavatsky and Jane Roberts.

Perhaps he should have turned to Carl Jung, since few psychologists understood intuition better than Jung. In his autobiography, *Memories, Dreams, Reflections*, he recalled a conversation he had in 1932 with Chief Mountain Lake. The Native American chief of the Taos pueblos in New Mexico told the Swiss psychologist, "How cruel the whites are: Their lips are thin, their noses sharp, their faces furrowed and distorted by holes. Their eyes have a staring expression. They are always seeking something." This attitude seemed crazy to the Native American. "We think that they are mad." When Jung asked him why he thought that all the whites were mad, the chief replied, "They say they think with their heads. We think here," indicating his heart.[3]

Just as Native Americans believed in the Great Spirit, Jung felt that there was a cosmic consciousness, which he termed the collective unconscious. Jung was fascinated by Eastern and Western philosophy, alchemy, astrology, and intuition all his life. He even wrote a doctoral thesis titled *On the Psychology and Pathology of So-Called Occult Phenomena*. As mentioned earlier, he later postulated that individuals possess four types of thought: direct sensation, emotion, reason, and intuition:

Physical sensation	Example: the taste of an orange
Emotion	Example: feelings of elation or depression
Rational thought	Example: logic
Psychic	Example: intuition

According to Edgar Cayce, "Meditation is listening to the Divine within."[4] It is also the best way to tune into intuition. Everyone has this natural ability to some extent; however, most people tend to ignore intuitive feeling. Carol found this out one cold November morning. The college student was in the habit of bringing her laundry to the local laundromat about a mile away from her Boston apartment. Most of the time, the chore was uneventful. However, one afternoon as she was about to put her wet laundry into a dryer, a thought flashed into her mind, "Don't use that dryer." Stubbornly, she closed the dryer door and put her last two quarters into the slot. When she pushed the knob on the dryer, nothing happened. It was broken. After lugging a heavy pillow case of wet laundry back to her apartment, she decided to pay more attention to her hunches.

Carol's experience is typical of intuition. It comes in a flash. Almost immediately people discount it, feeling it is imagination. In fact, intuition will almost always feel like imagination. However, with practice, it is possible to tell the difference, since intuition is really a message from a higher source. Sometimes that source is the higher self, spirit guides, or even God. If the person is ready, he or she will quickly respond to intuition.

For instance, Richard, an insurance executive and a devotee of Sai Baba who practiced meditation, asked for guidance at a turning point in his life. When he lost his job, he wondered what was in store for him as he was driving along the highway. He was very discouraged—that is, until he looked up and saw a billboard sign that said in huge letters: "We have big plans for you!" He instinctively knew it was a sign from God—not just an advertisement for a bank. A few months later, he found a better job. While faith plays an important role in intuition, so does meditation. Richard was a regular meditator, so he readily "knew" that he was receiving guidance from a higher source. Meditation stills the thinking mind and allows the spiritual contact with what Dr. Carl Jung called the collective unconscious.

Meditation also improves health. Dr. Herbert Benson, author of *The Relaxation Response*, discovered that meditation can lower blood pressure, reduce insomnia, and alleviate many other physical ailments. Now, more and more psychologists are advocating "mindfulness," a term coined by Dr. Jon Kabat-Zinn. The founder of the Stress Reduction Clinic at the University of Massachusetts Medical School was first introduced to meditation by Philip Kapleau, a Zen missionary. He then studied with other Buddhist teachers such as Thich Nhat Hanh and Seung Sahn and the Insight Meditation Society.

In 1994, Kabat-Zinn's book *Wherever You Go, There You Are* introduced many to mindfulness. According to Kabat-Zinn, "Meditation is the only intentional, systematic human activity which at bottom is about not trying to improve yourself or get anywhere else, but simply to realize where you already are."[5] His best advice: "Breathe and let be."

What actually happens in meditation? The mind shifts from the waking or beta brain waves to the alpha state of relaxation. This is the peace place where our natural intuition awakens. This hypnotic state of mind is absolutely natural. It is the exact same state of mind as your daydreams. Humans naturally enter into a daydream frequency every one to two hours during the waking day. Many people call it zoning out, fogging out, or drifting away. Daydreaming and meditation essentially transfer the individual from what psychologists term "left-brain" activity of the rational mind to the "right-brain" world of intuitive knowledge.

Psychic and medical medium Edgar Cayce recommended daily meditation to open the intuitive mind. He also advised the practice of meditation at the same time and place each day. For optimum results, sit or lie with back straight, so the psychic energy can travel directly up the body.

INSTRUCTIONS FOR RELAXATION MEDITATION

Set aside a regular time for meditation. It is best to start with five minutes and work your way up to a twenty- to thirty-minute period. Begin with a prayer and surround yourself with white light. You may wish to lie or sit on a cushion or mat used only for that purpose. Yogis believe that a meditation cushion is a buffer against unwanted earthly influences.

Sit or lie down without a pillow, so that your spine is straight. Then focus on soft music such as *Tibetan Bowls*, *The Eternal Om*, or *Silk Road*. Allow your body to relax. Each time your mind wanders, attend to the music. Eventually, you will enter a light trance state as the body relaxes. With regular practice, the meditator shifts from the waking state of beta brain waves to the relaxed state of alpha waves.

What actually happens in meditation? As the physical body becomes peaceful, the astral body can loosen from the physical body. Once the astral body is detached, the meditator can visit higher realms to make contact with loved ones, guides, and angels. With sincere effort, the meditator is welcomed to the higher planes: first, the higher mental plane, the Buddhic plane, and finally Nirvana. Often there is an inner feeling of clarity, sometimes accompanied by visual or auditory sensations—perhaps seeing vivid colors or hearing spiritual music. With practice, meditation can be a reliable form of contacting the Other Side.

INTUITION EXERCISES

Week-Ahead Exercise

Once a week, after meditation, take a moment to tune into the future. Write down five events that you think will transpire in the upcoming week. These events can be personal, such as Aunt Polly will call or the boss will be out of the office on Monday. You can also tune into world events, such as the stock market will go up or down this week. Simply allow the information to come. Remember, it will seem like your imagination at work—at least at first. Just be patient and allow the information to come intuitively.

Telepathy Exercise

Obtain five sets of Zener cards which parapsychologist at Duke University use to test telepathy and clairvoyance. If you wish, you can make your own Zener cards. Simply draw the symbols shown on white three by five index cards: Make up five sets. Then shuffle the twenty-five cards. Have a partner pick one and concentrate on it. See if you can predict which card your partner has in his or her hand. If you wish, you can also do this exercise with ordinary playing cards.

Scanning Exercise

Most people, with a little practice, are able to pick up the energy field of the body. Choose a partner to practice on. First, with one hand, make a slow sweep of the body of your partner. Begin at the top of the head and slowly crisscross deliberately down the body to the feet. Note any hot or cold spots, and when you finish, ask the person if there is any significance to the hot and cold areas. Often there will be places that have imbalances either in the past or present. For example, a sluggish thyroid, a heart condition, a backache, or even an old fracture may register as a hot or cold spot. Describe what you are feeling. As you share the information with your partner, ask for feedback. Then switch and allow the other person to scan your energy field. Again, take time to share information and give feedback.

CHAPTER FOUR

Developing Clairvoyance

It is one of the commonest of mistakes
to consider that the limit of our power of perception
is also the limit of all there is to perceive.

—C. W. Leadbeater

In 1996, reporters asked Jimmy Carter what was the most unusual thing that happened while he was in office. He said that a plane went down in Zaire with top-secret information. Desperate to locate it before the Russians did, US intelligence called in a psychic. As soon as he went into a trance, he gave the longitude and latitude of the location of the plane. With no time to waste, jet fighters were dispatched to those coordinates. Fortunately, a US jet arrived about twenty minutes before the Russians. That psychic was Uri Geller.[1]

Geller has the ability to heighten his intuition and tune into higher invisible frequencies. He was born with the ability to see psychic energies. Often, developing psychics learn to see clairvoyant images in their mind's eye first. Then when sufficient development occurs during meditation, they see the etheric lights and spirit people with their eyes open. Since the etheric world vibrates at a higher frequency, it may be easier to "feel" it rather than see it clairvoyantly.

However, if you wish to see the aura, you need to open the third eye through a regular practice of meditation. Once the meditator establishes a regular practice, he or she will begin to feel more peaceful within. Often the meditator begins to experience what the Hindus call siddhis, referring to paranormal abilities. When this occurs, it is not unusual to see spiritual energy, which vibrates at a higher frequency than the physical body.

As mentioned previously, there are actually seven vehicles: the physical body, its etheric double, the astral body, the lower mental body, the higher mental body or manas, the soul or buddhic body, and the atma or Divine body. According to theosophy, the manas, buddha, and atma form the soul, which each person brings with him or her from lifetime to lifetime. When breath ceases, the person sheds first the physical vehicle with its etheric double, and then the astral body. The final battle is between the lower mental and the higher mental bodies. If there is a strong attachment to earthly existence, then lower mind draws the person back to the wheel of life. For those who have conquered the lower mind, there is no need to reincarnate.

As people spiritually mature, they sometimes get glimpses of the spirit world out of the corner of their eyes with their peripheral vision. They may also see pinpoint lights. These lights may be white, blue, or purple, and they are usually the size of a dime. These lights are actually the astral bodies of spirit in the room. The clairvoyant is usually seeing the high point of the spirit aura. Many report this phenomenon as they enter a darkened room or close their eyes to go to sleep.

When the seeker's clairvoyant ability becomes stronger, the outline of spirit becomes clear. Then one can tell if the spirit is male or female. Note also any unusual features such as the outline of a feather headdress or a turban. Once outlines are established, it is possible to see the whole spirit. At this point of development, a clairvoyant can give an accurate descriptions of the spirits that are present to the sitter. Again take time to note an unusual features, such as scars, jewelry, or apparel.

The founder of theosophy, Madame Helena Blavatsky, had this type of unusual clairvoyant contact with ascended masters. She trusted the masters Moyra and Koot Hoomi implicitly. For instance, when she lived a poor existence in Apartment 7 at the Rue du Palais in Paris, she was told by her Master to go to an apartment and turn over what little money she possessed to a total stranger. The obedient seer did as she was instructed. When she knocked at the door, a very surprised gentleman opened it cautiously. When Madame Blavatsky gave him the money, he was most grateful. She had arrived just in time to save an impoverished man from committing suicide![2]

Children also have uncanny abilities. Some are even born with clairvoyance. Cyril Scott's book *The Boy Who Saw True* is the diary written by a child in 1885 who had clairvoyant gifts and was able to see spirits. However, this candor caused more than a few misunderstandings. When a woman visited the family, the clairvoyant youngster saw a strange-looking man above her shoulder. He innocently asked the woman, "Why have you got an old gentleman sticking to you?" He described him for her, and when he mentioned a red mark (a scar) on his cheek, she involuntarily replied, "Why that was Mr. ——," and looked at him uncomfortably. A few days later she questioned him about it, and that was when he discovered that not everyone saw these visions.[3] Sadly, the psychic child suffered many such indignities. While he wished to help others, he later allowed his wife to publish his diary—but only after his death.

The young boy possessed the gift of second sight and gave an excellent demonstration of objective clairvoyance. There are also mediums who possess a form of objective clairvoyance called x-ray in which the person becomes transparent and the conditions of the organs are made visible to the practitioner. Though rare, it has been used by mediums such as Rev. Andrew Jackson Davis and Dr. Hewitt of Boston, Massachusetts, who practiced in the early 1900s. Since he worked with medical doctors, he was able to get his patients into the Massachusetts General Hospital when necessary. He also received formulas for patients from spirit doctors and chemists.[4]

Scientists have also taken note of clairvoyance. In 1911, Dr. Walter John Kilner published a medical study of the "Human Atmosphere" or aura. He believed that seeing the aura could be a diagnostic tool. He developed a method of using the blue coal-tar dye or dicyanin as filters in "Kilner Goggles," used to train the eyes to see electromagnetic radiation outside the normal spectrum of visible light. According to Dr. Kilner, he was able to see what he called the Etheric Double, the Inner Aura, and the Outer Aura.

Aural photography has also been popular in Europe. In 1939, Russian electrical engineer Semyon Kirlian and his wife, Valentina, developed Kirlian photography. They noticed that when the electrodes were brought near a patient's skin, there was a glow similar to that of a neon light. Their work was unknown until 1970, when two Americans, Lynn Schroeder and Sheila Ostrander, published a book titled *Psychic Discoveries behind the Iron Curtain*. This is when Americans were first introduced to the process used in the Eastern bloc.

Dr. Thelma Moss of UCLA was intrigued that Russian and eastern European scientists were able to photograph the corona discharge glow at the surface of an object subjected to a high-voltage electrical field. Early in the 1970s, Dr. Moss and Kendall Johnson at the Center for Health Sciences at UCLA did their own research. With the aid of Kirlian photography, they were able to photograph the aura around a leaf. The experiment was called "the Phantom Leaf Effect." First, the Kirlian photographer took a picture of the energy field around a leaf from a healthy plant. The portion of the leaf was then "cut off," and another picture was taken. The second photograph still showed an energy pattern, as if the leaf were a whole one.

About the same time period, Peter Tompkins and Christopher Bird experimented with plants and their consciousness. Their research resulted in the 1973 book *The Secret Life of Plants*. They even used a polygraph on plant stimuli, a technique that was pioneered by Cleve Backster. The book details experiments that would indicate that plants do have feelings. The authors further state that the authorities are unable to accept the idea that emotional plants "might originate in a supramaterial world of cosmic beings which, as fairies, elves, gnomes, sylphs, and a host of other creatures, were a matter of direct vision and experience to clairvoyants among the Celts and other sensitives."[5]

Clairvoyant, C.W. Leadbeater, would have undoubtedly agreed with such research. In 1907, he published *Occult Chemistry: Investigations by Clairvoyant Magnification into the Structure of the Atoms of the Periodic Table and Some Compounds.*

Charles Webster Leadbeater.
Courtesy
www.spiritwritings.com.

The book was written with fellow Theosophists, Annie Besant and Curuppumullage Jinarajadasa, In *Occult Chemistry,* the chemical elements were assessed through clairvoyant observation in experiments carried out between 1895 and 1933. "The book consists both of coordinated and illustrated descriptions of presumed etheric counterparts of the atoms of the then known chemical elements, and of other expositions of occult physics."[6]

In the late 1980s, the author invited a Hartford Kirlian photographer to her parapsychology class. In the course of the evening, Barbara showed over fifty slides taken with Kirlian photography. For example, the aura of a healer was much larger than that of an average person. It was also amazing to see the aura of an average subject expand several inches when the person was holding a crystal.

Vedic astrologers have been aware of the aura force for centuries. In India, Vedic astrologers use gems and metals to strengthen the aura during adverse astrological transits. Gemstone therapy is now being used in the West as an alternative practice to strengthen the body and help resolve emotional issues. Hindus believe that by wearing gemstones close to the body, the aura is strengthened. They feel that when the aura is strong, the mind and body can heal itself. Each gem affects the aura differently. For instance, amethyst and clear quartz crystal are universal healing stones. Diamonds are for love and personal clarity. In India, emeralds are prescribed to calm the mind and soothe eye afflictions, while sapphires are used to protect against depression, and rubies are advised for courage.

Psychic Edgar Cayce recommended lapis lazuli, a deep-blue semiprecious stone, to enhance the psychic ability. For physical health, rose quartz is good for the heart, and emeralds are healing for the eyes. One cautionary note: Be sure to cleanse gems before wearing them by placing them in the sunlight or moonlight for a day. An alternate method: Soak them for a day in salt water made of one cup of sea salt to four cups of spring water.

Once crystals are cleansed properly, they can be placed in your meditation room or spiritual altar. Other items, such as pictures of Jesus, Buddha, or Ascended Masters, can be placed on the altar as well. Once you have set up your sacred space, you are ready to do trataka or candle meditation. In the East, gazing on a candle is said to open the third eye and stimulate psychic abilities. With regular practice, people become more sensitive to the etheric world as they stimulate their third eye.

Candle Meditation

Say a prayer of protection such as "The Lord's Prayer" or "Hail Mary." Surround yourself mentally with white light. Then call on your guides. If you do not know their names, call on Divine Mind or Infinite Intelligence to be present.

Next find a comfortable position that will allow your back to remain straight. You may sit in a chair with your feet on the floor. Be careful not to cross your legs. Place a candle on a table opposite you at eye level, about twelve to eighteen inches away. If you have long hair, you may wish to tie it back, or place the candle an arm's length from view.

Light the candle and gaze steadily into the flames for thirty seconds or so. Then close your eyes and allow your mind's eye to follow the afterimage. Try to hold the image in your third eye as long as you can. If the image moves away from your gaze, remain calm and concentrate on bringing it back into your mind's eye. Allow your consciousness to remain steady, focusing on the image of the flame.

Try the exercise three times at first. For maximum benefit, practice this exercise at the same time and place each day. Gradually lengthen your meditation time from five to twenty minutes as you become more comfortable. Many students start to see a jumble of faces. This sea of images is actually the first level filled with the newly arrived deceased. Often they seek communication. However, do not tarry in this realm. Go higher until you reach the summer land to connect with departed loved ones.

Don't be surprised if you do not recognize all the faces. When I first reached this sphere, I met an older gentleman in spirit who was sitting in a wheelchair. He said, "I am your relative." Next to him was a tiny spirit lady holding out a purple flower. She added, "This is my name." Later I found out that my great-grandfather, a diabetic, had lost his lower leg the year before he died—his housekeeper's name was Violet!

CHAPTER FIVE

Reading the Aura

*The clairvoyant is simply a man who develops
within himself the power to respond to another octave
out of the stupendous gamut of possible vibrations,
and so enables himself to see more of the world around him
than those of more limited perception.*

—C. W. Leadbeater

Edgar Cayce saw auras all the time—a gift that saved his life. One day as the psychic was about to get on an elevator, he noticed that the people staring at him had no auras. Startled, he stepped back. Within seconds, the elevator cable snapped. Everyone aboard was killed!

Fooling a clairvoyant is difficult, since the aura does not lie. Once when I was doing a clairvoyant reading for a well-dressed Russian lady, I sensed an unusually wide aura, which indicated someone with great influence. I said to the interpreter, "I don't know what your aunt does for a living, but she is very famous." Her niece nodded and said, "Yes, Aunt Olga is a famous opera singer." On another occasion, a white-haired woman came to the office. As she removed her winter coat and hat, I saw a long line of spirits behind. "You must be a medium," I exclaimed. "Yes," the New Britain woman murmured, "but I wasn't planning to tell you!"

The aura has three basic aspects—color, size, and texture. Colors in an aura can vary from red to ultraviolet, with white, black, and gray mixed in. For instance, when Edgar Cayce saw gray—the color of doubt in the aura of a middle-aged teacher, he gave this advice: "You have become fearful of the thing to which you have entrusted your inner self. There arise some smears of white coming from your higher intellectual self and from your spiritual intents and purposes."[1] To a young nurse with green, blue, and occasional streaks of red in her aura, Cayce made this observation: "I would not want to be around you when you do the streaking [of red] and most people who know you feel the same way, for when you let go, it is quite a display of temper."[2]

The colors in the aura tell much about the individual's personality and temperament.

To begin, **red** indicates vitality. Red generally is seen in the aura of athletes and those who like to be physically active. However, too-much red may create anger, though with compassion, red may turn to rose, a color of love.

The next color on the spectrum, **orange**, is also a high-energy color. It can indicate pride and success. People who have a great deal of orange possess confidence. They are outgoing and are good at sales and public speaking. People with an abundance of orange in their auras can really get things going. However, too-much orange may signify overconfidence and stubbornness.

Yellow, on the other hand, looks to reason, since it is the color of the mind. Teachers, counselors, and lawyers have an abundance of yellow in their auras. Often they love to be informed and make good communicators. Bright, golden yellow indicates confidence. However, pale yellow denotes a timid nature. No wonder cowards are called "yellow"!

Green is the middle color of the color spectrum. It represents harmony and denotes compassion. Doctors, nurses, and social workers usually have a lot of green in their auras, as do mothers of young children. If the shade of green is a deep emerald green, the person may excel in the medical field. However, if there is a "slime" green streak in the aura, watch out for jealousy. Once I observed two friends who were at odds develop a streak of yellowish-green in their auras. Within minutes, they began to argue—just as I made my way to the door!

The next color, **blue**, indicates a high mind. Blues can vary from blue-green, which likes to help in a practical way, to true blue, which is the color of an idealist, to the deep cobalt blue of a clairvoyant. Many a minister has blue in his or her aura. These people are honest and have good judgment. However, too-much blue can create extreme introversion of a recluse.

Finally, the last color is **purple**. At one time in history, only royalty could wear this beautiful color. It still is rare to see in the aura, since it is the color of deep devotion to God and spiritual healing. Edgar Cayce believed that the color purple in the aura could also indicate change and indecision. Once the decision was made, the purple would settle into blue. With this thought in mind, a light purple would indicate a change is coming, but the person doesn't know it yet. On the other hand, a deep dark purple indicates there is change of which the individual is fully aware.

The other basic colors—**white**, **black**, **brown**, and **gray**—also show up in the aura. White indicates purity; while black can be negativity. Gray, a combination of black and white, indicates doubt. Brown is seen in the aura of earthy, practical types and can indicate a materialistic attitude.

When a clairvoyant observes an aura, there is usually more than one color. Combinations of colors influence the person. For example, many police officers and firemen have the blue of service combined with red, indicating a preference for physical activity. Deep kelly green combined with cobalt blue is a healer—not so much a medical healer, but a spiritual healer, such as a Reiki practitioner.

The size of the aura is also important. When people are depressed, they pull their aura in. Reverend Gladys Custance saw extreme evidence of this in the aura of an elderly woman who took a bus from Boston for a psychic reading on the Cape. When Mrs. Custance looked into her long-time client's aura, she saw nothing. When she asked her guide, "the Professor," for advice, she saw a window shade pulled down. Not wishing to alarm the dear lady, the medium feigned illness. Less than a week later, the woman without an aura died!

Sometimes a client just can't make a decision. When a thirty-year-old married mother of a two-year-old boy came to see me, there was a bright streak of red zig-zags close to her head. "You can't seem to make a decision. One day you want another baby, and the next day you don't. You need more time to make a decision" was the advice given.

As noted above, as the clairvoyant begins to tune into the aura, he or she will describe color, shades, and shapes. Once you have established the aura, notice also variations in the aura over time as clients come for annual readings. For example, a person's aura will lighten considerably over time if his/her health has diminished. In the case of one client who came in from North Carolina for a reading, her aura had gone from bright colors of yellow, green, and blue to very pastel shades. When the change was mentioned, the attractive middle-aged mother of four nodded sadly, "I have just been diagnosed with M.S."

Cancer may sometimes be seen as black dots in the aura of a body. For instance, medical intuitive Tina Zinon saw "a million black dots" in her client's aura. The woman had stage 4 cancer. Fortunately, the cancer was removed by the client's surgeon.[3]

Of course, clients do not always heed the clairvoyant's advice. When the author was asked about a client's father, she saw a dark spot about the size of a quarter on his back. She advised the woman to tell her father to see a physician immediately, and there would be no problem. For some reason, her father did not go to his doctor, and he died a year later of skin cancer.

It takes years of training to be an accurate medical clairvoyant, but it is worth the effort. Most fledgling clairvoyants do well just to see the aura. Later, as their skill advances, they can tune into color, size, and texture. For beginners, start with the chart below and then add your message.

Colors in the Aura

Red	Vitality, physical strength—but too-much red, anger
Orange	Confidence, pride—but too-much orange, very sensual
Yellow	Intelligence, reason, sense of humor; pale yellow, timid
Green	Harmony, fair; slime green, jealous
Blue	Idealistic, spiritual—but too-much blue, reclusive
Dark blue	Conservative, responsible; overwhelmed by responsibility
Black	Negative or depressed
White	Pure at heart
Gray	Doubt
Brown	Materially minded

Aura Exercise with Dowsing Rods

Dowsing is a method that has been used for centuries to locate water and track energy. To do this exercise, obtain a pair of L-shaped copper rods. Hold the rods by their handles (the cylinder part of the rod) mid-chest height—one in your right hand and one in your left hand. The rods should be eighteen to twenty-four inches apart. Stand about fifteen feet away from the person. You may state your intent silently. You can simply say, "A might God-Force guides me in finding _____'s aura." Then walk very slowly toward the person. When the rods react by crossing, you will have found the outer edge of the person's aura. Then ask the person to think of a very holy person—for example, Jesus, Mother Mary, or Saint Michael. Try the exercise again to see if the aura has expanded.

CHAPTER SIX

Spirit Guides

*All the phenomena of mediumship are due to the
operation of spirit power.*

—Silver Birch

Tibetan guide;
artist: Rev. Phyllis Kennedy.
Author Collection.

Spiritual healers, mediums, and shamans are not alone in their task. With right intention, they attract spirit guides. As Silver Birch, the spirit guide of London medium Maurice Barbanell, explained, "All the phenomena of mediumship are due to the operation of spirit power."[1] Barbanell, by the way, was the founder and editor of a weekly Spiritualist newspaper, *Psychic News*.

The spirits of Native Americans often work with mediums such as Maurice Barbanell, and British medium Estelle Roberts had Red Cloud as her guide. American medium Ethel Post Parrish worked with the spirit of Silver Belle. American psychic Richard Ireland communicated with Crowfoot. While few Native Americans were understood by early settlers, they had a vast knowledge of the spirit world. Apparently, many have chosen to help from the Other Side, rather than return to this world.

Native Americans used many shamanic methods for healing members of their tribe. The shaman often journeyed to the world of the ancestors, so the sick could be healed by spirit helpers. They also used smudging to clear sacred space as well as to banish negative energy from the body. They frequently used desert sage, white broadleaf sage, juniper, pinon (sometimes in resin form), sweet grass, copal (in resin form), mugwort, lavender, and sacred tobacco. They would make smudge sticks with herbs or use loose herbs burned in a shell. The types of healing arts and spiritual ceremonies performed vary from tribe to tribe. Here are some of the common Native American traditions:

Animal Totems: Birds and animals are considered to be totem messengers offering spiritual guidance and emotional and physical support. Often the shaman will journey to send the correct power animal for the patient.

Sweat Lodges: The Native American sweat lodges are used for purification rituals to clean and heal the body, mind, and spirit.

Dreamcatchers: These are sacred nets made to catch negative spirits and protect one from nightmares.

Journeying: The shaman goes into a trance state in order to enter a realm beyond the earth. By journeying, the shaman gathers knowledge and performs healing.

Smudging: Smudging involves the use of herbs such as sage or sweet grass to purify the energy.

Medicine Wheel: This is a circle used for guidance; each direction of the medicine wheel offers its own lessons, color association, and spirit animal.

Talking Sticks: The tradition of passing a stick from speaker to speaker so that opinions could be communicated in a respectful manner.

Healing Amulets: Shells, crystals and gemstones, rattles, feathers, animal skin, and even bones used as lucky charms can be amulets.

Soul Retrieval: A shaman journeys with the intention of finding a person's lost life essence, which is returned to the client.

Extraction: The shaman, with the assistance of spirit helpers, removes negative energy.

Once, when queried regarding the change called death, Silver Birch replied: "Similarly there is weeping when people die in your world, but there is rejoicing in ours. Death means that the life has served its purpose, or should have done, and the individual is ready to enjoy all the tremendous richness and beauty that the spirit life has to offer."[2]

One cannot help but wonder why so many Native Americans assist mediums here and abroad. While the early settlers viewed them as a savage race, they actually possessed a sophisticated knowledge of the spirit world, which they termed "the happy hunting grounds," and God, or "the great spirit." Native Americans were also experts in prophecy and shamanic medicine. Many of their number who were slaughtered by the white man have chosen to take on the spiritual duty as protector for those who wish to walk between the two worlds. Frederick Harding explains, "The Indians, as Spirit Guides, must keep away and out of the mediums' aura and range of instrumentality, mischievous entities who are attracted by the operating line of manifestations."[3] In other words, the energy of mediums may attract good and negative spirits. Therefore, Native Americans in spirit have the job of repelling mischievous spirits.

In many ways, Native Americans were more spiritual than their white counterparts. It wasn't until 1848 that Spiritualism arrived with the rappings of the Fox sisters. Soon American Spiritualists were introduced to the use of spirit communication in healing by Rev. Andrew Jackson Davis. He was the first medical clairvoyant and trance healer. His guide was the spirit of the ancient physician Claudius Galenus (AD 129–200). Galen was well known as the Greek physician who attended the Roman emperor Marcus Aurelius. His principal interest was in human anatomy, but Roman law forbid the dissection of humans, so he performed anatomical dissections of animals. He was also interested in philosophy, and he wrote a treatise titled *That the Best Physician Is Also a Philosopher*. He also wrote *On the Diagnosis and Cure of the Soul's Passion*, which was an early attempt at psychotherapy.[4]

The Poughkeepsie seer first encountered the spirit of Galen when the medium was in an out-of-body state. He experienced what Spiritualists call traveling clairvoyance, and was transported to mountains some forty miles away. There to greet him were master guides—first, Marcus Galen, who discussed talked the healing power of nature. Next, the spirit of the Swedish seer Emanuel Swedenborg (1688–1772) appeared. When Swedenborg stepped forward from the ethers, he predicted that Davis would become "an appropriate vessel for the influx and perception of truth and wisdom."[5]

Fortunately, Davis took the advice of spirit and became a medical clairvoyant. The young medium was soon able to accurately diagnose medical disorders. Two times a day, Andrew Jackson Davis went into trance to contact Galen in order to diagnose and prescribe treatments. While he was in a trance state, the patient's body became transparent before his third eye. As he peered into the body, Davis described how he could see clairvoyantly inside it: "Each organ stood out clearly with a special luminosity of its own, which greatly diminished in cases of disease."[6]

At first, the medium required the services of hypnotist William Levingston and worked with New Haven doctor and magnetizer Dr. Silas Lyon, whom he convinced to become his personal hypnotist. Davis asked Livingston to enlist the services of Rev. Fishbough, a New Haven Universalist minister, as his private scribe. According to Fishbough, it would take Lyons three or four minutes to induce trance. When the process was complete, Davis would go into a convulsive shock. "For four or five minutes, he would remain silent and motionless, although occasional convulsive movements of his body might occur. He would then become cataleptic—his body cold, rigid, insensible, his pulse feeble, and his breathing apparently suspended."[7]

Davis became a prolific author, eventually channeling thirty books. The process was a slow one, since Davis first had to be put into trance, and then Fishbough had to be there to write down Davis's words verbatim. "For fifteen months, Dr. Lyon, his magnetizer, repeated each sentence as he uttered it, and the Rev. Fishbough, the scribe, took them down, restricting himself to grammatical corrections only."[9] The series of lectures resulted in a 700-page book, *The Principles of Nature, Her Divine Revelations, and a Voice to Mankind.* In its pages, spirit explained to readers that "The Divine Mind is the Cause, the Universe is the Effect, and Spirit is the ultimate Design."[8]

At the age of sixty, the medical clairvoyant graduated from the United States Medical College in New York. He spent the last years of his life in Boston, where he practiced medicine and maintained a small bookstore to sell books and herbal cures. At his death on January 13, 1910, he left a legacy of more than thirty books that had started with *The Principles of Nature, Her Divine Revelations, and a Voice to Mankind.*

By the time Davis passed to spirit, another American medical-trance medium, Edgar Cayce, was on the horizon. The two mediums have much in common. Both were dedicated to healing others; both were trance mediums who used hypnosis for a spell. When Cayce consulted a local hypnotist, Al Layne, to help him regain his voice, he made contact with a guide known as "the Source."

Cayce discovered this ability to diagnose illness early in life. "He was struck on the base of the spine by a ball in a school game, after which he began to act very strangely, and eventually was put to bed. He went to sleep and diagnosed the cure, which his family prepared and which cured him as he slept."[9]

As an adult, he developed a loss of speech. Al Layne put Cayce into a trance in order to diagnose the condition. According to his guide, "Cayce's voice loss was due to psychological paralysis and could be corrected by increasing the blood flow to the voice box. Layne suggested that the blood flow be increased, and Cayce's face supposedly became flushed with blood, and both his chest and throat turned bright red."[10] After several treatments, Cayce was able to have full use of his voice.

The Sleeping Prophet was also successful in curing his wife, Gladys, of tuberculosis after the doctor had given up. However, the Cayces did not trust the Source enough to apply this advice to their second child. Sadly, they lost the baby boy due to this reticence.

When another relative, Hugh Lynn Cayce, was blinded in an accident, the parents carefully followed spirit guidance and saved the eyesight of their six-year-old son.

While unorthodox, Edgar Cayce was ahead of his time. He was the first to apply a holistic approach to treatment. His cures ran the gamut from salt packs, poultices, and hot compresses to color healing, magnetism, vibrator treatment, massage, osteopathic manipulation, dental therapy, colonics, enemas, antiseptics, inhalants, homeopathics, essential oils, and mud baths: "Substances used included oils, salts, herbs, iodine, witch hazel, magnesia, bismuth, alcohol, castoria, lactated pepsin, turpentine, charcoal, animated ash, soda, cream of tartar, aconite, laudanum, camphor, and gold solution. These were prescribed to overcome conditions that prevented proper digestion and assimilation of needed nutrients from the prescribed diet. The aim of the readings was to produce a healthy body, removing the cause of the specific ailment."[11]

When a reporter contacted Cayce, he explained to the gentleman that he somehow had the ability to easily go into the intuitive sleep when he wanted to, and that this was different from how he went to sleep normally like everyone else. As the Source explained, "When asked the mechanism of the readings via the sleep method, they were told that it happened via the capabilities of the subconscious mind."[12]

Up until 1924, most of the questions were mainly about medical issues. Then Arthur Lammers, a wealthy printer and student of metaphysics, began to ask questions regarding astrology and reincarnation, followed by astrological influences and references to past life, which were added to the readings for the rest of his life. In 1925, the Source instructed that the Cayces move to Virginia Beach, Virginia, where the sand's crystals would promote swift healing. He followed the counsel and moved to Virginia Beach, where he remained until he had a stroke brought on by overwork. He died in 1945.

While Cayce's guides preferred to remain anonymous, simply referring to the group of spirits as "the Source," medium Harry Edwards received the names of his famous guides. He worked with the spirit of Dr. Joseph Lister, the physician who first demonstrated the use of an antiseptic in surgery in 1865. Edwards also contacted another noted scientist, Louis Pasteur. It is interesting to note that Lister and Pasteur—two scientists known for advocating antiseptic practices—were personal friends. Both suggested that surgeons wash their hands and sterilize their instruments before operating. They supported one another's efforts: "When Pasteur was publicly honored at age seventy by his medical peers, he turned and bowed his head towards Lister, saying: 'The future belongs to him who has done the most for suffering humanity.'"[13]

Almost a decade after Edgar Cayce's death in 1945, Harry Edwards was asked by a member of the Archbishops' Commission on Divine Healing what he believed to be the power behind spiritual healing. He replied in 1954, "I believe: that spiritual or divine healing, being the same thing, comes from God. That healing is directed to the sick through God's healing ministers in Spirit, who are part of the heavenly host."[14]

British healer Rev. Steven Upton now works with the spirit of Dr. Lister. Upton started developing his healing mediumship in 1977 and over the following seventeen years practiced this on a regular basis in a number of Spiritualists' National Union (SNU) churches. Since then, he attended the Arthur Findlay College, where he now serves as a tutor specializing in trance, in particular trance healing. The popular presenter has worked in Canada, Denmark, Dubai, Egypt, Finland, France, Germany, Holland, Iceland, Ireland, Italy, Norway, Spain, Sweden, Switzerland, and the United States.

John of God is another medium who heals with the help of spirit guides. In fact, he attracts many deceased physicians as guides, such as Dr. Oswaldo Cruz, Dr. Augusto de Almeida, and Dr. José Valdivino. The medium was born to a family who rarely had enough to eat, but he had the gift of clairvoyance. In his early teens, he saw the spirit of a radiant woman who told him to visit the nearby Spiritist center. The spirit was that of Saint Rita of Cascia. He followed her instructions and made his way to the center. John turned out to be an excellent trance medium. While he is one of the world's most powerful mediums, he remains humble. He often says, "I have never healed anyone. It is God who heals."[15]

When the entities work on the person requesting healing, they work to resolve the cause of the illness, not just the symptoms. For this reason, healing may require several sessions. According to Josie Ravenwing, "For some people, this may be a relatively fast and dramatic process, while for most, it takes place over time, continuing well after you have left Abadiânia, and sometimes requiring more than one trip to the Casa." She also adds, "The Casa entities will do all that they can to help and support our well-being, but they have also said on more than one occasion that they expect us to also do our part."[16]

In any event, the list of entities who work with medium John of God is impressive:

Dr. Adolfo Bezerra de Menezes (1831–1900)
A devoted physician, he believed that "A doctor is not entitled to finish a meal, nor to ask if it is far or near, when an afflicted person knocks on the door." After reading Allen Kardec's *Spirits Book*, he became a Spiritist.

King Solomon (770–931 BC)
He is associated with wisdom. According to the biblical accounts, Israel enjoyed great prosperity under Solomon's long reign of forty years.

Saint Francis Xavier (1506–1552)
Born in April 7, 1506, in Javier, Navarre (Spain), he was the son of a wealthy and noble family. He received an excellent education at the University of Paris. His friend Ignatius of Loyola convinced Francis Xavier to use his education as a Jesuit priest, which he did. He died on December 2, 1552, at Sancian in China.

Saint Rita (1381–1457)
She was born in the city of Roccaporena, Italy. When she was twelve, her parents arranged her marriage to Paolo Mancini, a quick-tempered man. After the death

of her abusive husband, the thirty-six-year-old entered the monastery of Saint Mary Magdalene. The spirit of Saint Rita is close to John of God. When she is at the Casa, people smell the scent of roses!

Dr. José Valdivino (dates unknown)
While little is known about his life, Dr. José Valdivino's photograph is in the surgery room of the Casa. When the spirit was asked about his life, Dr. Valdivino simply said that he was a protector of families. At the Casa, his gentle touch has healed many—especially paraplegics.

Dr. Oswaldo Cruz (1872–1917)
He is famous for wiping out yellow fever in Brazil. When the spirit of Dr. Cruz works with John of God, he will frequently request that wristwatches be removed because they disturb the current.

Dr. Augusto de Almeida (dates unknown)
This authoritarian spirit is reported to have been in the military and a doctor in past incarnations. He has pledged, "My phalange comprises not of ten, nor a hundred but thousands of Helping Spirits. I am the one who reaches to the very depths of the abyss to save a soul."

Dom Inácio de Loyola (1491–1556)
Saint Ignatius de Loyola brings the strongest energy to the Casa. During his life in Spain and Italy, he was known for many miracles: "For those who believe no proof is necessary, for those who disbelieve no amount of proof is sufficient."[17]

Types of Guides

Loved Ones	Deceased parents, grandparents, children, aunts, uncles, cousins, and departed friends
Spirit Workers	Helpers who are attracted by the choice of work
Temporary Guides	Guides who come in on an emergency basis, such as the spirit of a mechanic when a car breaks down
Protectors	Strong spirits who come in for protection. Mediums often attract Native Americans.
Joy Guides	Spirit children and beings who try to lighten our mood
Gate Keepers	Spirits who come to keep order in the séance room
Spirit Teachers	Highly evolved master souls who come back to teach higher knowledge
Spirit Chemists	Master spirit chemists and doctors who help to adjust the chemistry of the medium for spirit communication
Ascendant Masters	Guides such as Jesus, Saint Germaine, and El Mora who work for humanity
Angels	Loving and positive spiritual beings who have never incarnated

There are many ways to connect with spirit guides. Some people are introduced to their guide through a medium. Others may communicate with their guide in dreams. Often, those who meditate regularly begin to sense or see the presence of a spirit helper. Guided imagery can also help to connect with a person's guide. If you wish to contact a spirit guide, try the following exercise.

Meet Your Guide Meditation

Do the exercise in a quiet place when you have an hour to yourself. Turn off the phone and place a pen and a notebook at your side. Have another person slowly read this exercise to you.

In your mind's eye, go to your favorite place to relax. This may be the beach or your own backyard. See yourself in your favorite place to relax. Visualize every detail of the place—sight, sound, touch, even the taste. You are totally relaxed. Very, very relaxed.

Take a moment and imagine a white light just above your head. Visualize this white light shining above your head and gently coming down over your face, shoulders, chest, arms, hips, legs, and feet. Feel the protective warmth gently go down your body from your head to your shoulders; to your chest, hips, and legs; and to the bottoms of your feet. You are totally surrounded by brilliant protective white light.

In a moment—at the count of three—your guide will join you.

   One—you are peaceful.

   Two—you are excited about seeing your guide.

   On the count of three, but not before, you will see your guide.

   Three—your guide is right in front of you. Take a moment and look down at the guide's feet. What do the feet look like?

Slowly go up the body. What type of clothes does the guide have on?

See or feel every detail of your guide. Take a moment to tune in.

Now describe your guide in detail. What does your guide look like?

Does the guide have a name or symbol to give to you?

Pause.

Your guide has a message for you—a very vital message. Take the next three minutes to tune into this message, which will help you at this time in your journey here on the earth plane.

(At this point, play some soft—New Age—music for three minutes.)

Pause three minutes.

Now that you have received the guidance, thank the guide for being with you today. Send love from your heart to the guide.

On the count of seven you will awaken and remember every detail of your session. You will be able to write all the details clearly and easily. The more you write, the more you remember.

   One: You are rested.

   Two: You are beginning to wake up.

   Three: You will remember all details of your guide's message to you.

   Four: You feel well and happy.

   Five: You feel as if you have slept for eight hours.

   Six: You are alert. You feel energy in your body.

   Seven: You are fully awake. Eyes wide open.

CHAPTER SEVEN

Healing Angels

For he will command his angels concerning you
to guard you in all your ways.

—Psalm 33:8

Medical clairvoyants such as Edgar Cayce are guided higher forces. In Cayce's instance, his guide was the Source, who represented a group of spirits. There were also other guides, such as the Archangel Michael and Archangel Gabriel. Dr. Harmon Bro once described a visit from Michael after the group had been bickering. He said the room was charged with energy and the widows rattled from the power of Archangel Michael as he spoke though Cayce and criticized the group for the lack of compassion. Afterward, chastised, everyone just retreated to their own rooms," said Bro.[1]

Why would an archangel make an appearance? On one rare occasion, Edgar Cayce was giving a life reading for a four-year-old, Faith Hope Charity Harding from Trucksville, Pennsylvania. The child, who was known as "the Little Prophetess," was most unusual. According to Cayce, in past lives she had been Saint Cecilia, the patron saint of musicians, and before that, Elizabeth, the mother of John the Baptist. The Source told her mother that it was a privilege to care for Faith in this maternal experience.

Even though the windows were closed, a wind blew through the room so strong that it rattled the windowpanes and sent a pile of Gladys Davis's stenographer's notes flying across the room. "HARK, YE FRIENDS!" Cayce suddenly announced in a voice that had more force and fury than at any other time they could remember. Cayce continued. "Bow thine heads, ye vile ones of the Earth! Know what has been entrusted to thee! Live the life lest ye be counted accursed for being unworthy of the trust given thee!"[2]

The archangel wished to protect Faith and "keep strife from the door." Sadly, though her mother was a believer in Edgar Cayce, the father was not. Soon the sensitive six-year-old was caught in an acrimonious custody battle. In the end, her father won and raised his daughter in what he considered a normal life—without any trace of psychic training. If this had not been the case, the child might have manifested powers beyond even those of Cayce. She, who in a past life had been Saint Cecilia, no longer possessed the gifts of the spirit.

Of course, not all guides are the spirits of deceased saints and physicians. Angels also heal.

Noted clairvoyant Geoffrey Hodson (1886–1883) saw many types of angels. This former British officer was instructed in clairvoyance by Mary De La Middleton. He soon began seeing angels and nature spirits. In 1937, artist Ethelwynne Quaill, under his guidance, painted twenty-nine illustrations for his book *The Kingdom of the Gods*.[3]

According to Hodson, angels bring in the dawn and assist with sunset. They also are present to assist humanity in healing and ceremonies. Chief among the angels are the guardian angels, followed by the ceremonial angels and angels of beauty and art. Hodson often viewed angels in various-colored robes:

GROUPS OF ANGELS	COLORS WORN
Guardian Angels of the Home	Rose and soft green
Healing Angels	Deep sapphire blue
Angels of Maternity and Birth	Sky blue
Ceremonial Angels	White
Angels of Music	White
Nature Angels	Apple green
Angels of Beauty and Art	Yellow [4]

Flower A. Newhouse is another mystic who tunes into the angelic realm. She communicated with angels—those she calls the shining ones. She was born with extraordinary gifts of clairvoyance and believed early on in the reality of angels. She wrote her first book, *Angels of Nature*, in 1937. She spoke from personal experience of mysticism. In her work there is a vivid description of angels that brought them to reality for those who could not see them.

More recently, two sisters, Trudy Griswald and Barbara Marx, decided to try to communicate with angels. In 1991, the angels woke Barbara and requested that she get a pencil so that they could write to her. Three weeks later, Trudy had a similar unexpected experience. It was a miraculous beginning of countless sessions. Trudy was living in Connecticut; Barbara, in California; and they met halfway with the

Flower A. Newhouse,
BlessedBeyondBelief.
Public domain.

purpose of contacting their angels. After a fruitless first week, they began in earnest writing their book, *Angelspeake*, which has been an inspiration to many.

The angels spoke to both sisters with kindness and wisdom. According to the angels, we cannot see our own divinity: "Children, we are communicating with people all the time whether they know it or not. We often inspire persons to speak to you as an intermediary, because the message is urgent, clarity is needed, or a soul needs spiritual guidance."[5]

A few years later, in 1991, former Bell Laboratories engineer Stevan J. Thayer also connected to an angel. Much to his surprise, Ariel came to help with healing. This angel is known as the "lion of God" and is one of the four angels who guard the throne of God, as he explains in *Interview with An Angel*, which he coauthored with Linda Sue Nathanson. Thayer, a research psychologist, was seeking a medical alternative by entering a self-induced trance. His coauthor came to believe that she was in touch with an entity "identifying itself as Ariel," who instructed Stevan on healing using "integrated energy."

Psychic Kim O'Neill met her angel when, at a particular low point in her life, she was going through a divorce and was beset with financial difficulties—as she was about to lose her job: "I was at my desk at work and started to cry out that I have no husband, children, job, and I am miserable. I cried myself out, went home, and I had an angel appear to me, which scared the dickens out of me."[6] With the assistance of her guardian angel, who gave his name as John, Kim gradually rebuilt her life and wrote a book. According to the author and psychic, "All human beings, whether they know it or not, have at least two guardian angels to guide them through life." In *How to Talk with Your Angels*, she explains that spiritual communication will transform your life. She feels that it is "spiritual amnesia" that keeps people from building a life they love.[7]

It seems spiritual guides such as angels show up when we need them most. While some materialize, other guides who wish to assist come through dreams, meditation, or mental or even physical mediumship. Some may simply draw our attention through signposts. For instance, finding a penny can be an indicator that spirit is trying to get your attention. Why? A penny brings a much-needed message, "In God we trust." No matter the way your spirit guide makes his or her presence known, call on them for protection and guidance. Most of all, believe it is possible to make contact with guides.

Contact Your Guardian Angel

Ask for the angels to be with you.
Believe and trust that they will be there.[7]

A guardian angel is one assigned to protect you in this life. This is not a new concept. Throughout antiquity, people have believed guardian angels are here to protect and guide each person. Both the Hebrew Bible and the Old Testament refer to guardian angels: in Exodus 32:34, God promised Moses "my angel shall go before thee," and Daniel 10:13 talks about the angels Gabriel and Michael.

Angels come only to those with a pure heart. When they appear, they come as shining lights and with great compassion. While they cannot interfere with free will, they will stand by to guide you if you ask. For instance, when I was awakened in the night with severe stomach pains, I did not know whether to wake my husband to take me to the emergency room or try asking for guidance. Deciding to bide my time, I went downstairs to my office and began sincere prayer. Within minutes, a tall being of light appeared to my right. The angel said with great compassion, "Every effort will be made to keep you in the body." Reassured by my guardian angel, I fell into a deep sleep and felt much better in the morning.

If you would like to contact your guardian angel, try this exercise:

Situate yourself in a quiet place with a notebook and pen by your side.

Sit comfortably with your back straight.

Take three deep breaths.

Calmly say a prayer of protection such as "The Lord's Prayer."

Then begin a letter to yourself with the salutation: "Dear daughter (son). Begin the sentence, "You are a Divine child of God and . . .

Let your guardian angel finish the sentence.

See how to record your interaction as follows:

Date ....

Dear daughter (son): ....

You are a Divine child of God and ....

....

....

....

....

....

....

....

....

....

....

....

....

....

Clearing Negative Spirits

"You can't afford the luxury of a negative thought."
—Peter McWilliams

While it is best to avoid negative people and places, sometimes it is not always possible. Often, old homes come with what the British term "cohabitants." For the most part, the spirits of former residents are harmless. However, sometimes they are not.

Alma found this to be true when she moved into an older house in Arlington, Massachusetts, in 1963. She and her husband, Hank, loved the two-bedroom, gray Colonial. It was perfect for the childless couple. The location was close enough for Alma, a professional model, to make trips to New York for modeling assignments and was just twenty miles from the Boston base of Hank's aeronautics firm. Soon, Alma and Hank filled the rooms of their stately home with beautiful oriental rugs, lush silk curtains, and traditional décor. But however comfortable Alma made her home, she still felt a chill in one room. Every time she entered the pantry, she felt ill and experienced a cold breeze on the right side of her head.

Alma simply learned to ignore the unpleasant sensation—that is, until she joined a Spiritualist development circle in Boston. As she took classes with mediums Rev. Gladys Custance and Rev. Kenneth Custance, she listened carefully as Mrs. Custance talked about the DFs: dark forces. She began to suspect that a negative spirit might be at work in the pantry. When she asked her next-door neighbor about the history of the 1920s home, she was shocked to find out that the owner, an architect, had committed suicide there. Disheartened by the demise of his second marriage, he'd shot himself in the right temple in the pantry!

At first, Alma decided to pray for the disturbed spirit. Apparently, the spirit was a nonbeliever, since her prayers only served to irritate him. The spirit architect was constantly causing mischief of one sort or another. Lights would go out and temperatures dropped for no apparent reason. As if that wasn't enough, Alma felt a tug when she least expected it. One winter night, as she was going to her bedroom, a push from spirit was too much for the forty-five-year-old woman, and she fell down the narrow stairs. She was lucky to escape with only minor injuries.

However, a midnight trip to the emergency room at Mount Auburn Hospital convinced Alma that something must be done to oust her unwanted house guest. She called on the services of Rev. Kenneth Custance to exorcise her home. He and Gladys came and worked as a team to try to communicate with the negative entity. They went through the entire house from attic to basement, clearing the energy with incense and prayer. Finally, Kenneth spoke to the spirit and explained that he was indeed dead. "You no longer live here," said the minster. Then he commanded the spirit, "Go into the light." Fortunately, the exorcism worked and Alma had no further disturbances.

As one can see from this story, negative spirits do exist, and they can cause havoc. Often people suffer from diseases such as depression and addiction because of spirit attachment. Mediums such as the Custances have known about the work of Dr. Carl Wickland, author of *Thirty Years among the Dead*. At the turn of the twentieth century, Dr. Carl Wickland researched the topic with his wife, Anna, who was a medium.

Anna became a powerful medium after the death of her friend Mrs. Lackmund, who was also interested in the occult. The two made a pact a year before Anna's friend died that whoever passed first would return to communicate with the other one. They decided to use the sentence "Spirit return is true" as a test. Mrs. Wickland was most happy to receive this message, which contained the evidential phrase from the spirit of her departed friend: "Anna, spirit return is true. I will develop you. Go on with the work of obsession." Shortly after this, she appeared to Mrs. Wickland again at a materialization séance, giving unmistakable proof of her identity, and repeated her former words: "Spirit return is true. Go on with the work of obsession. I will develop you."[1]

Gradually, Mrs. Wickland attracted a little spirit girl named Pretty Girl, and Movilia, an Eskimo medicine man. The medium also had the spirit guide named Silver Star, who was a Chippewa Indian. She was born on an Indian reservation near Shell Lake in northern Wisconsin in 1883. When she was four, she passed to spirit due to a head injury. According to Silver Star, "We Indians are sent to earth to guard mortals because we know the law of protection, and so we serve others. Serving is progression in the spirit world."[2]

With the assistance of these spirit guides, Anna Wickland was able to see the Other Side, though some of these spirits were quite negative. Through his wife's mediumship, Dr. Wickland could communicate with the spirits who possessed mentally ill patients. As Anna looked over his shoulder, he tried to guide the disturbed entities "to possessing the spirit world." When this was not successful, Dr. Wickland used a low-level dose of electricity to rid the patient of the "obsessing spirit."

He shared his work in his 1924 book, *Thirty Years among the Dead*. According to Dr. Wickland, sensitive people have to be on the guard against negative spirits who want to inhabit a mortal body. Often the spirit of alcoholics still crave a drink and will hang around a local tavern with the intention of possessing the body of a drunken patron. That is why so many alcoholics suffer from blackouts. They are literally possessed.

While mediums have known about spirit attachment for years, it is just now being taken seriously by psychologists such as Dr. Edith Fiore, author of *The Unquiet Dead*. The clinical therapist was surprised to find that her patients had memories of past-life trauma, which she chronicled in her 1978 book, *You Have Been Here Before*. In 1987, she wrote about spirit possession in *The Unquiet Dead*. The psychologist believes that the spirits of deceased individuals can cause psychological and even physical problems when they attach themselves to living persons. According to Dr. Fiore, as many as seventy percent of her patients had spirit attachments.

Dr. and Mrs. Carl Wickland.
Wolfer Printing, 1924, public domain.

She realized that spirit attachments were especially strong with alcoholics. In the fall of 1983, a thirty-five-year-old computer analyst came to Dr. Fiore for advice. Peter said he felt he was a "bundle of nerves" and often drank for relief. He was also no longer attracted to his lovely young wife, Betty, and worried that he might have homosexual tendencies. Dr. Fiore found that several entities had attached themselves to Peter. His uninvited guests included a very bitter spirit, Joseph Biddle, and the spirit of David, whom he had picked up in a San Francisco bar. Sadly, David had been a satanic worshipper and was attracted to Peter because he had had a fleeting interest in Satan as a teenager. In addition, Peter was weak while under the influence of alcohol.

The patient also had a fun-loving spirit of a small-time singer, Eddie Vineburg, who he attracted in a bar in Sacramento, California. He even had a female entity, Laurie, who did not like to have sex when David was with his wife. It took many sessions to rid Peter of these negatives spirits. Dr. Fiore was able to do so with hypnosis and therapy. While the road back to health was a difficult one for Peter, he finally reached his goals: "For several sessions following Laurie's departure, Peter reported that his sexual relationship with Betty had continued to improve. His self-confidence and work performances remained strong. And his drinking problem had vanished."[3]

While enlightened psychologists such Edith Fiore are just now willing to acknowledge the presence of spirit attachments, shamans have been aware of possession for centuries. Dr. Alberto Villoldo, author of *Shaman, Healer, Sage*, believes that it is possible for spirit attachment to cause physical and psychical problems. When his book first came out in 2000, he flew to New York to attend a publisher's conference. Understandably, the Cuban-born author was nervous about promoting his book. However, Villoldo had a stroke of luck when the head of the publishing company introduced him to the attendees. The president told the group that he had once had a problem with alcoholism and had been cured by a shaman trained by Dr. Villoldo. Curious, the author called his former student to ask about the healing. The shaman told him that she had seen the spirit of the publisher's alcoholic father attached to him. When she told the spirit to leave, he did, and so did his son's desire for alcohol![4]

Not only do spirits attach themselves to people, but they also linger in public spaces. I found this out when I did a séance for the cast of the play *Blythe Spirit* at the Long Wharf Theater in New Haven, Connecticut. The cast looked forward to the postplay séance; however, a few members were concerned some of the spirits might stay behind. "That is not a problem," I said, "I will cleanse the theater after everyone leaves." To do so was quite a job for me, my husband, and psychic Ceil Lewonchuck. It literally took over an hour to smudge the space and clear the energy. Many negative spirits hovering in the corners of the Long Wharf had to be firmly told, "You do not belong here. Go to the light."

Shamanic Cleansing
Exercise

While it takes a great deal of energy and expertise to be able to clear large public spaces, the technique is a simple one. If you wish to clear energy in your office or home as a way to create a happier space, set a date with spirit. For example, some healers like to clear their spaces during the full moon. Always begin with a prayer of protection, such as "The Lord's Prayer" or the "Native American Prayer" (available at the end of the chapter). Then call on your spirit guides to be present. Next, visualize an angel in each corner of the room. If you are trained in Reiki, you can put the Reiki power symbol in each corner. Then, use a sage stick or a stick of incense such as sandalwood or Nag Champa to cleanse the room. Native Americans prefer to burn sage in a shell and to use a feather to direct the smoke.

Whatever method you wish to create smoke, it is important to hold a positive intention as you do the clearing. Try mentally sending the thought, "This room is full of pure and holy energy. Keep a sacred focus on what you are doing, and remain mindful throughout the process."

Start by smudging yourself before you work on the room. Simply hold the stick about ten inches from the top of your head and then slowly go down the one side, under each foot, and then back up the Other Side to the top of your head. Pay attention to your breathing. Make it slow and relaxed. Allow the smoke to do its work.

Then cleanse each of the four walls, with the intention of clearing the room and its contents of any negative or stale energy. Take time to notice how the smoke behaves and flows around specific objects. By being fully aware, you can even see the movement of energy as the room clears. When you are finished, intuitively check to see if there are any areas that need more cleansing, such as your desk or doorway. You may wish to open all the windows in the room to freshen the air afterward. If you are burning sage in a shell, then return the ashes to the earth by burying them.

THE LORD'S PRAYER

—Jesus of Nazareth

Our Father, who art in heaven,
Hallowed be thy Name,
Thy kingdom come,
Thy will be done,
On earth as it is in heaven.

Give us this day our daily bread.
And forgive us our trespasses,
As we forgive those
Who trespass against us.

And lead us not into temptation,
But deliver us from evil.

For thine is the kingdom,
And the power, and the glory,
For ever and ever. Amen.

NATIVE AMERICAN PRAYER

—Anonymous

Creator, Great Mystery,
Source of all knowing and comfort,
Cleanse this space of all negativity.
Open our pathways to peace and understanding.
Love and light fills each of us and our sacred space.
Our work here shall be beautiful and meaningful.
Banish all energies that would mean us harm.
Our eternal gratitude.

CHAPTER NINE

Hands-On Healing

Do not fret over the ignorant person;
surely they have not had the opportunities which illuminated your path.

—Chico Xavier

Very little is known about depossession in the United States. It is far more popular in South America. There are 3.8 million Spiritists in Brazil alone who believe in healing with spirits.[1]

The Spiritist movement was exported from France. In its heyday in the mid-1800s, it attracted attorneys, doctors, army officers, scientists, engineers, and educators. According to its founder, Allen Kardec, "The spiritual world is in constant contact with the material world, each reacting constantly on the other." Unlike other Christian sects that believe in an afterlife, Spiritists feel it is possible to communicate with the Other Side of life through mediums.

One of the most noted mediums in Brazil was the late Chico Xavier (1910–2002), who was a frequent guest on television programs. His mediumship began with a message from his deceased mother regarding his sister, who was plagued by insanity. The mother advised her seventeen-year-old-son to study the works of Allan Kardec. As the young man read *The Book of the Spirits*, he wondered, "Was it true as Kardec explained that obsession will one day be recognized as a cause of mental disorders?"

As Xavier studied the religion, he realized that he was a natural medium. He began to channel books through a process called "psychography." In the 450 books he produced, the spirits covered a wide range of topics, including religion, philosophy, literature, and science, as well as condolences to families. The revenue from his books, estimated at fifty million dollars, was donated totally to charity.

While Brazil's most celebrated Spiritist, Chico Xavier, is not well known in the United States, two other mediums, Jose Arigo and John of God, have been researched by American author John G. Fuller, who wrote about Arigo's healing work in *Surgeon with a Rusty Knife*. "For most, his [Arigo's] hand began almost automatically scribbling a prescription at incredible speed, as if his pen were slipping across a sheet of ice. Occasionally he would rise, place a patient against the wall, wipe the paring knife on his shirt again, drive it brutally into a tumor or cyst or another eye or ear, and remove whatever the offending tissue was, in a matter of seconds."[2]

How did he do this? The surgery was the work of an accomplished surgeon from spirit. Arigo first met this guide in a vision. According to his autobiography, around 1950, "One day he felt that the voice that had been pursuing him took over his body, and he had a vision of a bald man, dressed in a white apron and supervising a team of doctors and nurses in an enormous operating room."[3] This spirit identified himself as "Dr. Fritz." Dr. Adolf Fritz, a German doctor who died in 1918, performed the operations and wrote prescriptions.

Sometimes it is not necessary to physically operate to correct an ailment. Some psychic surgeons accomplish the task by operating on the spirit or etheric body. The surgery there would correct the physical ailments, since the etheric is a template for the physical body. This is how George Chapman (1921–2006) accomplished his psychic surgery; the medium worked in a trance state, much like Arigo. He also chose not to charge for his services. While Arigo channeled the spirit of Dr. Adolf Fritz, Chapman channeled a deceased doctor named Dr. William Lang (1852–1937), who had been an ophthalmic surgeon at London's Middlesex Hospital. In addition, the medium channeled spirit guides Ram-a-din-i and Chang Woo.[4]

Chapman, by the way, was not a natural medium. He joined the Aylesbury Fire Brigade after serving in World War II. After his premature daughter Vivian died, he tried to communicate using a Ouija board. The spirit of his mother came through as he placed a glass on the alphabet board. "Prompted by what was happening, the next step in George's progress was developing trance mediumship, sitting for three hours each day. In these periods he accomplished astral travel and made contact with both his mother and Vivian."[5] Eventually, he spoke with a spirit who gave his name as Dr. Lang.

In the book *Healing Hands*, author Bernard Hutton himself is described as being treated by Dr. Lang and saved from possible blindness. The experience made him a believer in the healer, who took no money for his work. According to Hutton, Dr. Lang operated on the spirit body, leaving the physical body untouched. "The healing technique used by Dr. Lang was to gently separate the patient's spirit body from the spirit form apparently translated into improvements in the physical form in relatively short order."[6]

His cures were nothing short of miraculous: "In 1974, a physician directed Joseph Tanguy to George. This young man was suffering from a malignant tumour in the brain, and after an unsuccessful operation was told that he had only six months to live. Distant healing was commenced immediately and was followed up by a spirit operation by Dr. Lang in December. After two further consultations, Dr. Lang advised that the disease had virtually disappeared."[7] George Chapman died in 2006 after sixty years as a healer.

The best known of the British healers was Harry Edwards. He strongly believed in prayer as well as the laying on of hands. A printer by trade, Edwards was surprised when a medium told him that he would make a good healer. She was right, since he was successful in his attempts at healing almost immediately. For instance, when a woman with twisted hands and immobile feet was wheeled into Edwards's healing room, he put the woman at ease and took her hands. "He put his hands on her knees and he worked them, and it is as if his hands were going into the joints and massaging and loosening them. He was such a good healer."[8] Her companion was amazed to see the woman, who had been in a wheelchair, walk out of the office without even the aid of a walking stick. Edwards died in 1976, but the Harry Edwards Healing Sanctuary carries on his healing legacy.

Fortunately, there are still some great healers in the world. Many consider John of God to be the greatest medical medium alive today. He was born João Teixeira de Faria on June 24, 1942, in Abadiânia, southwest of Brasília, the capital of Brazil. As a teenager, John of God had a vision of Saint Rita of Cascia, who told him that he was a healer and that she would always help him as long as he did not charge for healing. Spirit doctors take over his body and are able to perform healing while the medium is in a trance state. Thousands line up every Wednesday, Thursday, and Friday at the Casa to pass before the medium to receive advice from spirit on their health and other pressing issues.

In some cases, invisible surgery is needed, and in other instances, the surgical instruments come out. If one is selected for an invisible operation, he or she is told to sit in a room in the Casa and meditate. When John of God enters the room, he will channel energy and bless the person by saying, "In the name of Jesus Christ you are all cured. Let what needs to be done be done in the name of God." The medium tells people not to stop taking their medicine, and admits that not everyone he serves will be cured.

One woman, Jodi, told me that she'd had eye surgery when she was in Brazil. Apparently, the middle-age writer had been diagnosed with an eye problem that required surgery. "When I entered the room in the Casa for surgery, I didn't have time to think. John just asked if I would like him to heal my eye. When I nodded 'yes,' he quickly pulled out a surgical instrument. Before I knew it, he was operating on my eye." Apparently, he scraped the cornea of her eye. According to Jodi, the surgery on her eye was painless. However, she added, "I did feel some pressure, and my eye teared up and was sensitive to light for awhile." She followed John of God's instructions and did not read or watch television for two weeks. When Jodi visited her eye doctor in Chicago, he saw no need for surgical intervention.

Usually, surgeries are performed by people between the ages of eighteen and forty-five. When a patient cannot make the trip to Brazil, surgeries are performed on a surrogate patient. Such was the case for noted author Dr. Wayne Dyer. His eye doctor, Dr. Rayna Piskova, called him and said, "I am making a second trip to

Brazil to see John of God. I would very much like you to come as well; I can't emphasize enough how important I feel this is for you." Dr. Dyer wanted very much to go but he had a deadline to meet and was weak from his two-year battle with cancer, so Rayna went to Abadiânia to be his surrogate.

He noted: "In the morning I awake to a phone call from Rayna, who's also having surgery simultaneously with John of God in Abadiânia. She informs me that I need to go back to bed and sleep for the next twenty-four hours and treat this remote healing the same way as if I'd just had my gallbladder removed by a local surgeon."[10] He also drank water blessed by John of God and took the sacred herbs that were FedExed to him.

After the "spiritual surgery," Dyer found a large scar on the back of his neck, which he showed to his friend Reid Tracy. The scar disappeared in the two weeks' time; however, the healing was permanent. After the distance treatment, he was completely cured of cancer. When he died of a heart attack in 2015, he did not have a trace of leukemia in his body according to the coroner's report.

A man of great faith, Dyer believed, "With God, all things are possible."[9] John of God was trained as a medium in a Spiritist church. The Spiritists believe that paranormal power can be harnessed for medical use. In fact, there are fifty Spiritist psychiatric hospitals in Brazil offering inpatient and outpatient services that utilize an integrative approach to recovery, stressing the spiritual alongside physical and psychological therapies.

According to Dr. Emma Bragdon, the healers begin with prayer, and then trained practitioners make energy passes. "The actual energy work typically involves circumscribed gestures where the healer passes his or her hands three to six inches above the body of the patient, starting above the head and passing down the body to below the knees. Treatments last only a few minutes per person, during which time each patient remains seated, eyes closed, if possible."[11] If nothing else, patients appear to be more at peace.

During the twentieth century, dozens of Spiritist hospitals used a variety of means to treat patients' maladies. In fact, a 2011 article published in *Culture, Medicine, and Psychiatry* stated: "Brazilian Spiritist psychiatric hospitals provide an integrative concept for the treatment of psychiatric disorders, combining conventional psychiatric therapies."[12] While traditional medicine and drug therapies are offered, they include spiritual practices such as prayer, laying on of hands, and spirit release therapy. Spiritists believe in some cases that negative spirits take over the bodies of addicted or psychotic patients, so they have mediums on staff to rid the patient of spirit possession. The founder of the Spiritist movement, Allan Kardec, explained that negative spirits along with trauma from past lives are the chief causes of mental illness.

When I was in Brazil in 2007, I asked to be driven to a Spiritist hospital in Anápolis. Expecting a basement clinic, I was pleasantly surprised to see a block-long substantial structure. When I asked the driver, a former air force officer, if many people were healed, he answered, "Absolutely! My brother had a terrible drinking problem. He stayed in that hospital one month and has been sober for several years." Apparently, the daily energy passes, along with depossessions, work.

The Hospital Espirita de Psiquiatria Anapolis is not the only Spiritist psychiatric hospital on Brazil. There are fifty such institutions. These hospitals combine a spiritual approach to mental health along with medical and psychological remedies. Much of the work is done by spiritist practitioners who donate their services, which include laying-on-of hands, prayer, medical intuition, and the release of negative attachments. According to Avildo Fioravanti, the President of the Federation for Spiritism in San Paulo (FEESP), the centers have a ninety percent success rate in their treatment of addicts and severely depressed patients.[13]

Author in front of the Hospital Espiritade Psiquiatria, Anápolis, Brazil.
Courtesy Ronald Kuzmeskus.

Spiritual Healing

There are three basic types of spiritual healing. The first is often absent healing, and the most common type of absent healing is prayer. Churches of all religions recognize this form of healing. At the Harry Edwards Healing Sanctuary, prayers are sent out twice a day at 10:00 a.m. and 10:00 p.m. Another good resource for prayer is Silent Unity. People can call a number, and a staff member will pray with you using positive affirmations. Many people report that they feel a sense of peace after the session.

Never underestimate the power of prayer—especially group prayer. After Maggie's fourteen-year-old grandson was nearly killed in a car accident, the family was glad he was alive. However, their joy was short lived when his doctor told the family, "It looks like Jimmy is going to lose his leg." There was a small group from an inner-city church in the waiting room of the hospital. When they saw Maggie's distress, their leader approached her and asked if they could go to Jimmy's room to pray for him. She nodded, "Yes." The group formed a circle around the sleeping young man's bed and bowed their heads in prayer for about thirty minutes. The group came every day thereafter. The doctor, amazed by the boy's progress, saw no reason to amputate his leg.

The second type of healing, contact healing, involves the transfer of energy from one individual to another. It requires the same sincere faith and a true desire to heal as prayer healing. However, with contact healing, the healer's hands are actually placed on top of the patient's head or shoulders to conduct the flow of energy. Some healers place one hand on the recipient's forehead and another on the back of the neck. Contact with the head and shoulders is sufficient for the purpose of healing, but some training is advisable. Most Spiritualist churches offer training and certification in contact healing.

How does this form of healing work? According to the National Association of Spiritualist Churches, "The healer's hand or hands are placed upon the recipient's head, shoulders, or both, thus becoming a conduit through which this energy flows. The spiritual healer may be acting as a transformer of the spiritual energy to make it more readily absorbed by the recipient." While some healers will ask if they may place their hands on the afflicted areas, touching the patient other than the standard positions of head and shoulders and gently over the heart area is not necessary. In any case, it is important to ask permission to place hands on the person and to be careful where you place them.

The third form of spiritual healing is mediumship healing, such as that done by John of God. With mediumship healing, spirit doctors work directly with the patient to relieve symptoms. Often the medium will be in trance, but it is not always necessary. It is a rare gift that requires both expert mediumship and the help of altruistic spirit doctors.

Sometimes, despite a healer's best efforts, a patient may not be cured. There are many reasons for this. Chief among them is karma. This happened to be the reason for a young lady who was so severely crippled that she had to be carried into the ashram. Her mother, desperate for a cure, brought her to see Sai Baba, whom many in India considered to be an Avatar of God. As devotees watched him approach the girl, they prayed for a cure. While Sai Baba did give the girl some relief from her symptoms, she still could not walk. His disappointed followers asked Swami, "Why did you not cure the girl?" He said it was not possible because of her karma. In a past life as a soldier, she had tortured another as she was ordered to do. The person who gave the command was her devoted mother in this life!

In cases where there seems to be no immediate response to healing, it is best to leave the result to God. Try releasing the situation with this spiritual mantra:

Lead me from the unreal to the Real
Lead me from darkness to Light
Lead me from death to Immortality.

—Ancient prayer from the Brihadaranyaka Upanishad.

Remarkable Healings

Natural Forces within us are the true healers of disease.

—Hippocrates

Hippocrates, the father of orthodox scientific medicine, also gave credence to healing through laying on of hands: "It is believed by experienced doctors that the heat that oozes out of the hand, on being applied to the sick, is highly salutary. It has often appeared, while I have been soothing my patients, as if there was a singular property in my hands to pull and draw away from the affected parts aches and diverse impurities, by laying my hand upon the place, and extending my fingers toward it."[1]

Five centuries later, Jesus became famous for his hands-on approach to healing. People would travel for miles to see the healing rabbi perform his miracles. He made lepers whole, helped the lame walk, raised the dead, drove out negative spirits, and gave the blind sight. The Gospel of Mark tells of a most poignant miracle that took place in Bethsaida. When Jesus came into the town on the shore of Lake Galilee, he was asked to heal a man who had been blind from birth. Jesus created mud by mixing dirt with spittle, which he then placed on the man's eyes. In order to complete his healing, Jesus directed the man to wash his eyes in the Pool of Siloam. When the man did this, he was able to see for the first time. Jesus's disciples asked the master whether the cause of the blindness was due to the sins of the man's father or his mother. Jesus answered his disciples, "Neither this man nor his parents sinned, but this happened so that the works of God might be displayed in him. That it was neither, that the will of God be shown."[2]

Many later Christians, such a Cabeza de Vaca, a trader from Spain, were inspired by the example of Jesus. The Spaniard developed empathy for the native people in the Texas territory. His efforts to cure through Christian means were successful. Cabeza de Vaca writes that he and his companions used their Christianity as a means of healing. For example, "The very night we arrived, some Indians came to Castillo telling him that their heads hurt a great deal, and begging him to cure them. After he made the sign of the cross on them and commended them to God, they immediately said that all their pain was gone."[3] He used the sign of the cross as his symbol of healing, while the Indians used their "shamanistic" calabaza. He also writes that "at sunset, he made the sign of the cross on them [sick Indians] and commended them to God our Lord, and we all asked God as best we could, to restore their health, since He knew that that was the only way for those people to help us. And God was so merciful that the following morning they all awakened well and healthy."[4] Needless to say, Cabeza de Vaca gained quite a reputation as a faith healer in his time.

The Victorian era brought renewed interest in faith healing around the world. The leading healers in the United States included Phineas Quimby, Dr. James Newton, and Rev. Andrew Jackson Davis. In 1836, French mesmerist Charles Poyen came to Belfast, Maine. After attending Poyen's lectures, Quimby came to believe that disease was caused by false beliefs, and that through mesmerism (hypnosis), one could be cured.

The early hypnotists were believers in traveling clairvoyance. Using this technique, which is now known as remote viewing, trained clairvoyants could travel in their imagination to another location or even time period. Quimby was excited to learn that one of his subjects, Luther Burkmar, excelled in traveling clairvoyance. The young man, while in trance, could diagnose diseases and even give cures. The two teamed up and traveled throughout New England to give demonstrations of Luther's clairvoyance and promote hypnosis.

Quimby noticed that people were sometimes cured by their belief alone—a phenomenon that doctors now call the placebo effect. This changed the healer's perspective. If it required only belief for someone to be cured, then he reasoned, "Disease being in its roots a wrong belief, change that belief and we cure the disease."[5] According to Quimby, "If the patients admit that he tells them their feelings, then his explanation is the cure; and, if he succeeds in correcting their error, he changes the fluids of the system and establishes the truth, or health. The Truth is the Cure."[6]

Quimby also looked to the Bible for guidance and incorporated its teachings into his cures. He became convinced that seventy percent of illnesses were due to wrong belief: "The trouble is in the mind, for the body is only the house for the mind to dwell in."[7] This idea would become the genesis for his healing and the New Thought movement. Mary Baker Eddy was one of Quimby's patients who was cured by his mind cure. She later used his work as a model for Christian Science.

In 1859, Quimby opened an office at the International Hotel in Portland, Maine. People, many of whom had been diagnosed as incurable, flocked to his office from 1859 to 1865. For those who were unable to make the trip to Maine, he used his own gift of clairvoyance to diagnose at a distance. For example, he gave this accurate description of illness to Miss B: "You have a sort of dizzy feeling in your head, and a pain in the back part of the neck. This affects the front part of the head, causing a heaviness over the eyes. The lightness about the head causes it to incline forward, bringing the pressure on your neck just below the base of the brain, so that you often find yourself throwing your head up, to ease that part of the head. This makes it heavy, so it bears on the shoulders, cramps the neck, numbs the chest, so that you give way at the pit of the stomach and feel as though you wanted something to hold you up. This cramps the stomach, giving you a gone-feeling at the pit of the stomach. This contraction presses on the bowels and causes a full feeling, at times, and a heaviness about your hips, and a logy feeling when you walk."[8]

Dr. James Rogers Newton is another extraordinary healer about whom little is known. Olivia "Livy" Langdon Clemens, wife of author Mark Twain, was cured by this faith healer. As a teenager, Miss Langdon had become paralyzed due to a fall. Her wealthy father paid $1,500 to James Rogers Newton for Olivia. It should be noted that the doctor only charged patients who could afford to pay a fee of $1,000—the poor received healing for free. Dr. Newton prayed for a few minutes at Olivia's bedside. Then the girl, who had been bedridden for two years, took several steps. According to Mark Twain, Newton pulled back the shades and said, "Now we will sit up, my child. Miraculously, with a prayer, Newton aided Livy in walking a few steps."[9]

Dr. Newton believed that spirit magnetism may be used for healing. He was against anything that might restrict the flow of energy. For example, he warned that wearing garters makes feet cold and crippled limbs. He also advised his patients "to never sleep or sit with hands up to the head; it will cause heart disease. Consumption, liver complaints, and dyspepsia finally, he believed that spirit magnetism—the life principle—may be imparted from one to another, and is the only power to heal the sick."[10] He always stressed the "love principle," even for patients. He advised them, "Sorrow, grief, fear, or any extraordinary emotion, will cause disease; so to be well, be cheerful, and wear a pleasant countenance."[11]

Andrew Jackson Davis also believed that healing came from the Divine: "The Divine Mind is the Cause, the Universe is the Effect, and Spirit is the ultimate design."[12]

Davis was also the first person to diagnose and prescribe cures for individuals while he himself was in a trance state, about fifty years before Edgar Cayce. "In his writings about the human body and health, Davis described how the human body was transparent to him in this trance state. Each organ of the body stood out clearly with a special luminosity of its own which greatly diminished in cases of disease."[13]

Davis was able not only to diagnose but also treat illnesses. He practiced magnetic healing with good results. He often placed his hands in difference positions depending on the illness. For example, for asthma patients, he would place his hands on the spine and rub vigorously.[14] He also wrote prescriptions for medicinal purposes.

Fifty years later, Edgar Cayce became well known as a medical clairvoyant. Cayce would frequently connect illness to the mental and emotional states of the patients. In one reading he was quoted as saying, "Thus you can . . . [suffer] a bad cold from getting mad . . . [or] from . . . [cursing out] someone."[15]

Early in his career, Cayce naturally had doubts about his ability; however, his desire to help others overcame any reluctance to heal. He was called to Kentucky to heal his infant nephew, Tommy House Jr., who had convulsions that were so bad that his doctors had little hope. When Cayce went into trance, spirit gave the baby's vital signs and accurately described the condition of the body. Then the Source recommended a most unusual cure, belladonna. The decision to try this poisonous substance was left up to the boy's mother, Carrie House, since his father, Dr. House, felt he could not use such a remedy. She must have known Cayce's cure was her only chance of saving her baby, since she forced little Tommy to swallow the deadly nightshade. For the first time her baby fell into a deep sleep. In the morning he appeared rosy cheeked and had no convulsions that day—or any more in the days to follow.[16]

Fortunately, Edgar Cayce made a full-time commitment to doing readings for clients such as Elsie Sechrist. She consulted the trance medium in 1941 because she was told by doctors that she had only a year to live. The young nurse had been diagnosed with a heart condition. She received several readings in which treatment was outlined. According to Sechrist, there was an "instantaneous rapport."[17] Her reading from Cayce confirmed that the two had known each other 12,000 years ago in Egypt. She later wrote three books based on her study of the Cayce readings: *Dreams: Your Magic Mirror, Meditation: Gateway to Life,* and *Death Does Not Part Us.* She was active in the Edgar Cayce Association of Research Enlightenment Health Center & Spa (ARE) until her death at age eighty-three.

Psychics such as Cayce often receive requests for healing. Some do so with prayers; others use hands-on healing. Most Spiritualist mediums do both, since a healing is part of the Spiritualist tradition. Such was the case with Rev. Carl Hewitt, pastor of the Gifts of the Spirit Church in Chesterfield, Connecticut. He was doing a reading for a nurse, and as usual when he felt the energy go down, indicating that spirit was about to leave, he asked if she had any more questions. She surprised him by saying, "I would like you to heal my hand." Apparently, the woman had been out of work for over a year because her right hand was paralyzed. According to Rev. Hewitt, "I was already in an altered state of consciousness, so I put my hand on top of hers. I felt a tremendous amount of energy coming from my body."[18] After a few minutes, he let go of her hand, leaving the results to spirit. The next morning, he was pleased to receive a call from his client. She told the medium that she was able to write a letter with her right hand![19]

Many people possess the gift of healing through laying on of hands. One of the most tested healers in recent years was the late Dean Kraft, who discovered his ability to heal as a young man. At first he worked with family and friends. Then he worked with people who had severe need for healing—those suffering from ALS and cancer. For the next forty-one years he produced remarkable laying-on-of-the-hand healings, which he detailed in his book *A Touch of Hope*. "His abilities have been tested by scientific experiments at the Lawrence Livermore Laboratory and the Science Unlimited Research Foundation—and in one fascinating study, in 1975, he was repeatedly able to kill deadly cancer cells, sealed in glass flasks . . . simply by holding the flasks in his hands"[20]

Spiritualist medium Rev. Carl R. Hewitt.
Courtesy Rev. Hoyt Robinette.

CHAPTER ELEVEN

Afterlife Communications

Know that all healing forces are within, not without!
The applications from without are merely to create within a
coordinating mental and spiritual force.

—Edgar Cayce

Edgar Cayce did 14,000 readings in his lifetime. The majority of requests were for healing, which the "Sleeping Prophet" believed came from within. He also stressed that anyone who took the time to develop could become a channel for spirit. When friends requested a reading for the purpose of developing their psychic abilities, Cayce readily agreed to help them.

The first lesson that Cayce's trance guide gave was one on cooperation: "For these brought helpful experiences to many, and these activities may be applied in the present in the building of cooperation" (Edgar Cayce reading 3639-1). The Source stressed that lesson two could not be given until this cooperation was achieved. It took the group a year just to master lesson 1!

However, the group had enough loyal members to continue to meet for more lessons. Eventually, their sessions with Cayce became a book, *A Search for God.*

Lack of cooperation is a problem for many groups, not just the Cayce people.

Sadly, some Spiritualist circles break up because of lack of teamwork; however, those that manage to stay together may accomplish much. For instance, Boston medium Rev. Gladys Custance had a circle that met on Friday evenings for over forty years. When the author joined the group in 1969, it had expanded to about forty sitters, which included a several teachers, a rabbi, and two Massachusetts Institute of Technology professors. The older professor proudly told the group how he believed in the 1940s that the United States would have a man on moon. When his colleagues expressed skepticism, he pounded his desk, declaring, "In twenty-five years, I'll have a piece of moon on my desk!" Sure enough, one of the astronauts brought a moon rock as a gift to the professor!

Everyone in the circle was impressed by his anecdotes. It was confirmation that spirit did indeed guide the members. After a discussion period, the circle began to

Edgar Cayce on the couch in his office. *Courtesy of the Association for Research and Enlightenment, Virginia Beach, Virginia.*

meditate in earnest. The purpose was to relax with music as well as silence. As Mrs. Custance often reminded members, "Tension shuts the door to spirit." Once, relaxed by meditation, members of the group were instructed to "give impressions as they come to you." People would comment on how the room had become suddenly filled with people from the Other Side. Sometimes everyone would smell roses or lilacs. Many a night, the group saw blue, white, and purple lights swirl around the Commonwealth Avenue apartment. Almost everyone experienced a heaviness much like a helmet over their heads, as the healing energies worked to open the crown chakras and third eyes of fledgling clairvoyants and healers.

Healing is a very important part of Spiritualist ministry. Most churches include prayers for healing as part of their service. Prayers and affirmations were sent out during the development circle as well. In her private readings, Mrs. Custance never shied away from answering a question on health, but she did so in way that honored the medical profession. An astute clairvoyant, she could see illnesses before they manifested in the body. In such cases, she would wisely counsel clients to see a doctor. "If you have not had a check-up recently, it is time to see a doctor," she calmly advised.

Sometimes spiritual counsel was needed more than medical wisdom. For a twenty-eight-year-old woman consumed with anger toward her ex-husband, the medium wisely pointed out, "If you keep feeling angry, there will come a day when you have arthritis. It is better to let the matter rest." "Take time to pray," she told the mother of two young girls. While this may not have set well at the time, it was the best the medium could do. The woman did pray and eventually remarried.

Prayer was especially important for those in the group who wanted to be healers. She would give each one a list of ten or so names of people who had asked for healing. Then each day, the healer would be instructed to visualize each name and say a prayer for each individual. It was best to do this at the same time and place each day. The names were to be kept confidential.

Mrs. Custance was very professional. She never gave out the names of her clients. Since she was a trance medium, she did not have to worry about sharing the reading. Whatever she did remember, she kept in confidence. She also respected other mediums. Once when a client of noted medium Rev. Arthur Ford asked for a reading, she refused to book her until the Ford agreed to the session, which he readily did.

As science investigates medical clairvoyance, it is hoped that more people will take readings seriously. One of the first researchers to study life after death was Dr. Raymond Moody, who studied 150 people who had had a near-death experience. He listed fifteen common characteristics, which he discussed in his book *Life after Life*. Often, those who survive a near-death experience report hearing a buzzing sound or loud ringing, feeling a pull out of their bodies, and then experiencing the sensation of going through a tunnel of light. At the end of the tunnel, they see the spirits of deceased loved ones. At some point, they are told that it is not their time to pass over. Then they may feel a strong desire to return to complete unfinished family responsibilities. When they return, they exhibit change of consciousness, with the conviction that death is not the final step on the soul's journey.

Dr. Ebon Alexander had a profound near-death experience in 2008, when he contacted bacterial meningitis. He went into a coma and hovered close to death for a week. During that time, he was far from unconscious. As he later related, he was living intensely in his mind. The comatose man was guided by "a beautiful girl with high cheekbones and deep blue eyes" on the wings of a butterfly to an "immense void" that was both "pitch black" and "brimming with light," coming from an "orb" that interprets for an all-loving God.[1] The events that took place in the afterlife had such a profound effect on Dr. Alexander that he wrote a book about his experience—*Proof of Heaven*.

Scientists Dr. Gary Swartz, Dr. Craig Hogan, and Dr. Raymond Moody would agree with Ebon Alexander's belief in consciousness beyond the body. They have begun to take a serious look at the possibility of afterlife communication. Gary E. Schwartz, PhD, did considerable research on mediumship, documented in *The Afterlife Experiments*. In 2001, Dr. Swartz and Dr. Linda Russek conducted an experiment with mediums. They asked the question, Can mediums receive accurate information under laboratory conditions? The mediums were surprisingly accurate, with an eighty-three percent accuracy for the actual readings, which gave details both on the living and deceased.

While some of the received information was general, most of it was precise. For instance, using a medium, he was successful in contacting the spirit of parapsychology author Susy Smith. According to Schwartz, "Susy cooperated perfectly, even telling me portentously that I should check the tires on my car. It turned out that a few hours later I walked into the parking lot of my laboratory to find one of my tires had gone flat."[2]

As you can see from this example, mediumship is a three-way process involving spirit, medium, and sitter. Not every spirit is as persistent as Susy Smith, and not every medium is as receptive as those who took part in Dr. Schwartz's experiments; however, when the sitter is receptive, true communication is possible. In mental mediumship, spirit creates a link between the medium and the sitter's guides. The sensitive then picks up the messages by utilizing the five psychic senses that correspond to the five physical senses:

Psychic Senses

Clairaudience: Psychic hearing. The medium hears the voices from spirit, music, or other noises from the spirit world.

Clairgustience: Psychic smelling or tasting. A psychic may taste apple pie in her mouth or smell lilacs.

Clairsentience: Psychic feeling. The medium feels or senses the presence of spirit. Often this is accompanied by a change in temperature. Literally the hair on the medium's arms raises, or she may feel a chill down her back.

Clairvoyance: Psychic vision. A psychic will see spirit either as an objective in front of him/her or will see it in the mind with his/her eyes closed.

Psychometry: The ability to read energy by holding an object, such as a watch or a ring. A good psychic can pick up vibrations of the past, present, and future for the owner.

Psychometry is the easiest skill for a beginner. It can produce amazing results, as in the case of British medium Estelle Roberts. When Mr. Ewart Dudley placed a sealed envelope in front of her, she just felt the piece of folded textile. Then she was asked to use psychometry to ascertain the message written on the needle work, and the medium immediately felt the spirit of a woman take her hand to trace, "COME UNTO ME ALL YE THAT LABOR AND ARE HEAVY LADEN AND I WILL GIVE YOU REST. MARY BAKER."[3] Estelle Roberts correctly identified the needlework and quickly added, "also in the envelope are two lace fronts, which I used to wear with my low-necked blouses. One is square and the other triangular in shape. There is also a narrow strip of hand-worked lace, which was done by my mother, your grandmother."[4] She then tore open the envelope to reveal a picture of Dudley's mother—the spirit who had taken the medium's hand to trace the quote from Mary Baker Eddy!

As evidential as mediumship can be, not everyone wishes to consult a medium. There are other ways to get in touch with a loved one. Watch for physical signs such as orbs or flashes of light. For those who were handy in their earthly life, the spirit may play with electricity—turning lights, televisions, or appliances off and on. Once you sense the presence of spirit, relax and acknowledge their presence.

However, these dramatic events are not always present. A more common way to contact the spirit world is through dreams. That is how Rev. Arthur Ford discovered his psychic gifts—through a series of nighttime communications. When he was serving in the army in 1918 he began to have psychic dreams. "Later he began to hear the names of soldiers who within the next days would appear on the casualty lists. Their names were in exactly the same sequential order on the list as Ford had previously recorded the day before."

Larry Dweller was also introduced to mediumship through dreams. The author of *Beginner's Guide to Mediumship* had a dream visitation when he was fourteen: "One dapper gentleman dressed in a houndstooth suit and white spats appeared regularly in my dreams, usually delivering lectures on the importance of homework and imparting advice on how to get along with family members." Shortly thereafter he spied the dapper gentleman in a family album. It was his grandfather, who died in 1932.[5]

Spirits are often quite concerned about their earthly relatives. Prolonged and complicated grief can be as much a source of deep psychological pain for the mourner as the deceased. For example, Isabel Allende, in her book *Paula*, described her recurring dreams of her daughter who passed away at age twenty-eight. Frequently, Paula's spirit appeared dressed in a white nightgown and slippers. She urged her mother to stop grieving since it was holding Paula back.

Spirit contact in dreams is more common than most people realize, largely because they do not remember these dream visitations. Memory fades quickly once the dreamer is fully awake. It is best to record dreams before getting out of bed, so keep a notebook and a pen by your bedside. Sometimes a pen with a built-in nightlight is helpful.

Once you have written the dream down, take time later in the day to interpret it. Not every dream is a visitation from spirit. Some may be the product of a pastrami sandwich and a hot fudge sundae late at night! These dreams are of little consequence. Other dreams may be like reading yesterday's news as they flit from one event to another. Often the dreams are reviewing past events or trying to see future possibilities. This is particularly true of dreams in which the dreamer is shopping.

Psychic or lucid dreams are usually steady, clear, and detailed. Often these dreams have a significant purpose or a message for the dreamer. It is not unusual in psychic dreams to know that you are dreaming. Sometimes these dreams have an authority figure such as a priest, nun, teacher, or physician.

If loved ones appear, they usually look healthy and younger. Often the dearly departed will communicate telepathically without the need for speech. Sometimes they bring messages or symbols through. Here is list of the most-common symbols and their meanings:

Baby	New beginning
Book	Knowledge
Bridge	Connection
Car	Transportation
Clock	Time
Death	An ending
Moon	Mystical, feminine
Music	Harmony
Sun	Recognition, masculine
Telephone	Communication

In addition to common universal symbols, there are personal symbols that occur in dreams. For instance, if your grandfather smoked a pipe, then a pipe in a dream may represent grandpa.

Dream visitation can be a source of comfort—seeming more like a visit than a dream. According to Rosemary Ellen Guiley, author of *Dreamspeak*, spirit communication can be divided into three categories: the farewell, the reassurance, and the gift. Guiley explains, "Themes within these types of encounter dreams are the eternal bonds of love; forgiveness, blessings; assurances; gifts; and information about the Other Side."[6] It makes sense that loved ones wish to say a final goodbye.

Psychometry Exercise

If you wish to connect with a spirit friend or loved one, try psychometry. Hold an article that belonged to the deceased. Metal is especially good, so if possible use a watch or a ring. Then practice meditation, say a prayer, and see what comes into your mind through intuition. At first these thoughts may seem like imagination. However, intuition often started this way. Eventually, you will make a strong contact and receive stronger impressions. Try asking spirit an open-ended question such as, "How can this person improve their life circumstances or health?" When giving out health advice, always preface it with, "I am not a doctor, and I do not diagnose."

After-Death Communication Exercise

Many people report contact with their loved ones in dreams. They receive messages of reassurance and love. Spirits wish to let grief-stricken relatives and friends know that death is not the end of the relationship. Widows frequently report dreams of their departed husbands, urging them to go on with their lives. Also, it is not unusual for parents to be comforted by the appearance of their deceased child in a dream. Just seeing his or her face can be healing.

Sometimes mourners will contact a professional medium. While it is gratifying to make contact with your loved ones through a psychic or a medium, it is entirely possible to communicate with those on this side through dreams.

Before going to sleep, send the thought out to your loved one that you wish to be in contact. It could be a simple request, such as, "Please visit me in a dream," or "I would love to make contact with _____ in a dream." Then, let the thought go. Just have faith that when spirit is ready, he or she will come into your dreams. Allow them the dignity to come for a visit as they wish.

After making a sincere request, take a moment each morning to write down dreams, fragments of dreams, or simply thoughts that come. Otherwise, you are likely to miss vital details of the spiritual visitation. With time and patience, the veil between the two worlds will lift. When it does, date these dreams and underline the names of spirit loved ones for your records.

CHAPTER TWELVE

#

*The soul always knows what to do to heal itself.
The challenge is to silence the mind.*

—Caroline Myss

Medical mediumship is a special area that few mediums are willing to undertake unless they are working with a licensed physician. Most mediums who do wish to heal may choose to use Spiritualist healing or clairvoyance, which have been covered in previous chapters. The third method of medical mediumship is direct communication from spirit. Perhaps the best example of this method is Edgar Cayce, who was able to diagnose and prescribe as a trance medium with the help of his spirit doctors.

Spiritualist mediums also attract spirit doctors who wish to be of assistance. When they do, they may find that their clairvoyance sharpens. They begin to see health conditions in the aura. At first, the mediums may keep this information to themselves, especially if the medium does not have a medical background. However, more mediums such as Tina Zion, RN, do possess both medical and mediumship training. She uses mediumship to describe illness and treat the energy field. If she sees an illness, then she will refer the client to a licensed physician.[1]

According to Zion, "Intuition will always feel like your imagination." Since intuitive thoughts pop in without much effort, most people discount them. Zion advises that mediums in training learn to receive information without altering it. Often, intuition will come in the form of symbols, which can later be interpreted. With training and practice, Tina Zion believes, "We can positively manipulate our energetic body in order to see with x-ray eyes."[2]

Often, medical intuitives such as Zion can alert clients to illnesses in their early stages. For one social worker who came for a reading, early detection was a lifesaver. After I saw a gray area over one woman's left breast during a routine mediumship reading, the middle-aged woman left the office understandably shaken. However, she believed me when she was told, "You must see a physician immediately." Her doctor's early diagnosis of breast cancer made it possible to have the lump removed rather than losing her left breast—and five years later she is still cancer free. These readings are always difficult ones. Even though a medium should be honest about what he or she receives, it is also important to give the information in a thoughtful manner. When necessary, describe what you see without diagnosing—leave that to the doctors.

Some mediums are so passionate about healing that they become doctors—such as Andrew Jackson Davis and Douglas Baker. Also a few modern doctors, such as Mona Lisa Schulz, give medical intuitive readings. When Dr. Schultz does private medical intuitive readings, all she requires is the client's name and age. She then tunes into emotional issues, followed by a description of the physical body. Usually Dr. Schultz can tune into her patient within the first five minutes. In rare cases in which she cannot "read" the person on the other end of the phone, she gives a full refund.

More often, medical intuitives such as Caroline Myss prefer to partner with a physician. In the fall of 1982, Myss gave up her career as a journalist to start Stillpoint, a small publishing company dedicated to alternative methods of healing. At the time, Myss did not have any background in mediumship or meditation, yet gradually her own medical intuition emerged. For instance, she could be having coffee with a friend and she "knew" instantly if something was wrong. As word of her abilities spread, people were soon calling her for intuitive consultations. Two years later, she began working with Dr. Shealy. After a great deal of testing, Shealy concluded that Caroline Myss had the ability to diagnose illness with a ninety-three percent degree of accuracy.[3]

In 1996, she wrote the definitive book on chakras, *Anatomy of the Spirit*. The book goes through each of the seven chakras and explains their issues. For example, the first chakra corresponds to tribal energy of the group. "Misplaced loyalties or conflicts will most likely manifest in the lower part of the body, in afflictions like lower back pain." A woman of faith, Carolyn Myss believes, "The soul always knows what to do to heal itself. The challenge is to silence the mind."[4]

While Carolyn Myss began her work as an adult, some medical mediums, such as Anthony William, discover their gift earlier in life. When he was four years old, Anthony shocked family members when he announced at the dinner table that his grandmother had lung cancer. Later medical testing confirmed that his grandmother, who was symptom free, did have lung cancer. How did the child know? The medium explains that he received information from his spirit guides, who scanned the client's body and relayed the information to the medium.[5]

According to William, when other boys were playing sports, he was "constantly witnessing disease in the people around me and listening to Spirit tell me what's needed for them to get better."[6] By the time he was fifteen, talking to spirits became an everyday event for him. On one occasion, his spirit guides even gave instruction to fix his mother's car when the local mechanic was unable to do so. As with many budding mediums, William felt overwhelmed by his gift. Eventually, the young man accepted his destiny as a medical medium.

Nowadays, William readily dispenses advice on the root causes of a client's illness. He does this by scanning his clients for physical, emotional, and soul imperfections. "When I scan a client, fractures of his or her soul resemble cracks in a cathedral window. I can tell where the fractures are because that is where the light comes shining through."[7] In 2015, his book *Medical Mediumship* came out. He believes that those suffering from chronic illnesses, such as fibromyalgia or chronic fatigue syndrome, may be infected with the Epstein-Barr virus, which he terms "a secret epidemic." The book also contains recommendations for a healthful diet coupled with herbal supplements.

Medical mediums such as Williams often are able to detect illnesses in the aura before they can manifest in the physical body. For those who wish to pursue medical mediumship, begin by scanning the aura. Look for colors, textures, and patterns. Take note of any irregularities. Here are some examples of how illness may be seen in the aura by a trained clairvoyant:

Anxiety	Red ric rac (or wavy lines) in aura
Bladder infection	Red in pelvic area
Depression:	Gray or black over the forehead
Diabetes	Gray over the pancreas
High blood pressure	Red over the heart area
Jealousy	Slime green in the aura
Parkinson's	Washed-out, pale aura
Slipped disc	Black or gray over back area
Thyroid	Hyperthyroidism red over the throat
Hypothyroidism	Gray over the throat

Notice also the condition of the chakras. As a person approaches death, the upper chakra opens more, as the lower three close down. Sometimes the dying person will see relatives who are in the spirit world. This is natural as the sixth chakra (the third eye) opens, and so does clairvoyance. Simply allow the dying person to share his or her experiences. Be sure to reassure the person that he or she is not hallucinating, but instead seeing the Other Side of life.

That said, never give up trying to heal a person. Miracles do happen. Sometimes when the doctors can do no more, God steps in. Mary Sweeney found this to be true when she was put into an insulin-induced coma when the doctors believed that she was close to death from AIDS. Friends from the local Sai Baba center came and prayed during the weekend. When her doctors brought her out of the coma, she said that she felt much better. She even was able to go back to return to her job at a Hartford insurance company. Mary lived three more years—precious ones for her husband and two teenaged girls.

The first step in developing mediumship of any variety is to deepen the trance state. There are many ways to do this: sitting in a development circle, meditating, or using hypnosis. Trance can vary from a relaxed state to a fully unconscious state. The deeper the trance, the stronger the degree of spirit control. Andrew Jackson Davis, Edgar Cayce, Eileen Garret, and Kevin Ryerson are examples of excellent trance mediums.

Basically, trance is the result of focused attention. Edgar Cayce described following a pinpoint of light as he left the body. Other mediums simply feel that they have taken a nap. Students often ask, "How do I know I am in trance?" Here are some common signs:

- Heartbeat slows down.
- Breathing becomes slow and steady.
- Body temperature drops.
- Time perception is altered.[8]

In mediumship, trance is further aided by guides. Master guides always work with the student's permission. They never command. They never demand.

When hypnosis was becoming popular at the turn of the twentieth century, early hypnotists used it to explore medical clairvoyance. French hypnotist Charles Poyen became well known for this practice. One subject, Miss Gleason, an English weaver by trade, was a particularly gifted medical clairvoyant while in trance: "Usually she made her diagnosis, passing her hand over the patient's body, head downward, describing as she did so the various organs. She claimed the body became transparent and she could see the organs in detail."[9] With no medical background, she used simple terms to describe illnesses, such as "pimples on the liver." Miss Gleason was even known to diagnose at a distance by holding a lock of the patient's hair.

If you wish to use hypnosis to scan the body, try the following exercise. For best results, sit or lie in a comfortable position and have a friend read the material to you slowly. Afterward, get feedback on your accuracy.

Hypnosis Exercise:
Progressive for Body Scan

First, sit in a comfortable position. Keep your legs straight.

Now take a deep breath in through the nose and out through the mouth.

Do this three times. Relax your eyes.

Visualize a white lotus blossom serenely floating in a pool of aqua water.

Feel your eyes become completely tranquil as you watch the white blossoms floating.

Let this feeling of relaxation go into your forehead, erasing all cares.

Then let it gently go into the cheeks, chin, and throat. All tension is released in the throat.

Next, this relaxation flows into the shoulders, releasing all pressure in the muscles.

Now visualize this relaxation going down your right shoulder, to your right elbow, to your right wrist, to your right hand.

Completely relax.

Let this relaxation flow into your left shoulders, down your left arm, to your left elbow, to your left wrist, so your whole left arm is completely relaxed.

Then down the spine, so your spine is as limp and flexible as a piece of spaghetti.

Your shoulders, spine, and back are completely relaxed.

Your chest is relaxed. All tension is released from your shoulders, chest, lungs, heart, and stomach.

All organs are operating smoothly.

This relaxation goes into your hips, down the right hip, to the right knee, to the right ankle, so your whole right leg is relaxed.

Then down your left leg, to your left knee, to your left ankle, so your whole left leg is relaxed.

Your whole body is now relaxed from the top of your head to the soles of your feet.

Take a moment to tune into the body of _____, age_____.

Describe the physical condition of the person. Pause.

Start by going into the head area—brain, eyes, nose, and ears. Now go deep within the neck, throat ,and shoulders.

Pause.

Now go into the right arm from the shoulder to finger tips.

Describe what you feel.

Pause.

Then the left arm from shoulder to finger tips.

Describe what you feel.

Pause.

Bring your awareness to the chest, lungs, and heart.

Describe their condition.

Pause.

Continue throughout the abdomen, hip, and groin area.

Describe their condition.

Pause.

Go down the right leg from hip to toes and describe the condition. Then go down the left leg from hip to toes and describe the condition.

Now focus on the spine. Start at the neck and slowly go down the spine.

What is the general physical, emotional, mental, and spiritual condition of the person?

Pause.

Ask your guide to step in and give whatever message is needed to bring this person optimal health.

Pause.

Now you are ready to return to the present. On the count of seven, you will wake up feeling wonderful in every way.

> One: You are ready to return.
>
> Two: You feel rested.
>
> Three: You feel wonderful in every way.
>
> Four: You have peace of mind.
>
> Five: You are becoming more aware of your surrounding.

Six: You are back to your normal state.

Seven: Eyes wide open.

As you do this exercise, remember that you can describe only what you see. Most of the time, you will pick up old injuries, scars, and minor issues such as backache. However, it is important to explain that you are not a doctor and do not diagnose. If you feel that there are irregularities that could warrant medical attention, by all means, tell the person to consult a physician.

CHAPTER THIRTEEN

Healing Grief

Death, be not proud, though some have called thee
Mighty and dreadful, for thou art not so.

—John Donne

Death Be Not Proud is the title John Gunther chose for his book about his son, Johnny. In the book, Gunther recorded the true story of his teenage son's struggle to overcome a brain tumor. The story began when Johnny, a student at Deerfield Academy, experienced a stiff neck. His doctors were concerned enough to do exploratory surgery. When they discovered a tumor the size of an orange in his brain, his parents were shocked. Though recently divorced, they remained united in their determination to find a cure. They even consulted Canadian neurosurgeon Dr. Wilder Penfield and Dr. Max Gerson, noted for the "Gerson diet," a vegetarian diet with hourly glasses of organic juice.

All the while that John Gunther Jr. followed the strict regime, he remained selfless, wishing to spare his parents any worry in his last months on earth. He still tried to keep up with his studies and enjoy time on the Connecticut shore with his dreams intact. Even in his last few weeks, the brilliant young man hungered for knowledge. In the end, his father wrote, "Like a thief Death took him."[1]

After his death, Johnny was not forgotten. While his father, a world traveler and journalist, wrote a memoir, his devoted mother, Frances, wrote the epilogue. She reminded parents just how precious their children were: "Today, when I see parents impatient or tired or bored with their children, I wish I could say to them, but they are alive, think of the wonder of that!"[2]

It is never easy to say "goodbye." When a parent dies, the past is lost; when a spouse dies, the current life is over. But when a child dies, the future is gone. These events are life changing. The task of grieving can be made more bearable by the comfort of family, friends, and spiritual counsel. Their support, however well meaning, cannot take away the pain. Parents are the most anxious to communicate with their deceased child.

Just as their children experience stages of death, dying parents experience their own stages of grief. According to Dr. Elisabeth Kubler-Ross, the five stages of death and dying are:

1. Denial
2. Anger
3. Bargaining
4. Depression
5. Acceptance

Parents often feel numb at first; some may feel intense anger or depression. Eventually there is an acceptance of their loss. At this point, those with knowledge of the afterlife may wish to communicate with their child.

Many times the deceased are just as eager to let their family and friends know that they are all right. One of the most common communications from the Other Side is to assure those on earth that the departed are at peace. A medium often encounters spirits who just wish to say hello. Such was the case when I was at a local Barnes & Noble bookstore to do a book signing for *The Making of a Medium*. I heard a spirit say "Helen" and felt a grandmother's love go toward the young woman wearing a Manchester Community College sweatshirt. The girl looked confused when told, "Helen, your mother's grandmother has a message for her." After "Helen" spoke, the young lady just shrugged, "I don't even know the name of my mother's grandmother." Her great-grandmother stubbornly insisted, "Why don't you just call your mother and find out." Ten minutes later, the skeptic came back and told the group, "I just called my mother. Her grandmother's name was Helen!"

As one can see from this example, the so-called dead do wish to communicate with the living—sometimes even more so than those on earth. The bond is usually one of love; however, sometimes there is unfinished business. For instance, a widow contacted a medium, Lamar, to find her husband's will. The middle-aged man had recently died of a heart attack, and no one could find the will in his office. After the medium from Camp Chesterfield made contact with the spirit of the departed husband, he was able to tell the widow where the key to the husband's file cabinet was hidden. When she opened it, she was most pleased to find the will in question.

When someone dies a violent death, the soul may remain earthbound, not realizing that the body is dead. Just two months before the attack on the World Trade Center, Joyce Keller, a New York psychic, just happened to buy an apartment a thousand feet from the center. On September 11, 2001, she found herself in the unusual situation of witnessing the demise of the WTC and its aftermath. As spirits, the recently departed firemen and office personnel piled into her living room, and she spent the morning reassuring the many who had suddenly passed to spirit. One firefighter was surprised that he could fly with his boots on, not realizing he was dead. She and her husband, Jack, continued to help spirits cross over until early in the morning of September 12.[3]

Another difficult death is murder. I did a reading a few years back for a burly police officer. He came with a photo of an attractive, waiflike, blonde young woman, Katy. Immediately, I sensed that Katy's life had been taken from her, accompanied by a rush of anger—and I added, "She knew her murderer." Apparently, she had been brutally murdered by her on-and-off-again boyfriend. "I told her so many times not to go back with him," said the broad-shouldered police detective, wiping a tear from his eyes.

What are some ways to deal with grief? One is to acknowledge loss. That is why psychologists often feel that it is important to view the body, so the person knows that the loved one really did die. One distraught mother, Linda, sent her second husband to view her daughter's body and to make arrangements after the girl died unexpectedly. After the body was cremated, she had second thoughts. Within days after the funeral, the mother contacted a detective agency to search for the girl, believing that there could have been a mistake in identification, since her husband was not the girl's father.

According Dr. Julie Beische, director of the Windbridge Institute, an organization that studies mediumship under strict controlled conditions, she notes that unresolved grief can be the source for mental anguish and physical distress. Often, traditional psychotherapy can provide only minimal relief. She recommends that therapists combine mediumship readings with therapy: "The combination of traditional psychotherapy and mediumship readings may prove to be more beneficial than either intervention separated."[4]

When it comes to grief, true afterlife communication can be extremely healing. However, it may take the departed some time to adjust, just as it takes the living some time to accept the loss. If a mourner visits a medium too soon, the spirit may not have sufficient energy to manifest. Those who have recently lost a loved one can be very vulnerable and may need time to grieve before visiting a medium for the reassurance that the loved one has survived.

During the first three days after death, spirits frequently try to make their presence known to those they leave on the earth plane. It is not unusual for a medium to see the spirit of the deceased standing right next to their relatives as mourners pass by the coffin. Spiritualist mediums such as Kenneth and Gladys Custance helped parents, spouses, and friends connect with the departed by giving validation messages. Often they would describe the spirit, tell the manner of death and possibly give a name or initial, and then share a personal message from those on the Other Side of life.

Another Spiritualist medium, Rev. Arthur Ford, even gave both the first and last names of the deceased. For example, when he conducted séances for Rev. Sun

Spiritualist medium Rev. Arthur Ford from old newspaper clipping.

Myung Moon in 1985, he provided first and last names of the deceased: "In a sitting on November 1964, Ford said Fletcher mentioned Pieter Alexander, who had learned about Sun Myung Moon's ideas on spiritual growth."[5] Later, Arthur Ford conducted the first televised network séance when he made contact with the dead son of Bishop Pike in 1967.

Often the bereaved wish to make immediate contact with the Other Side. However, it is best to wait a month before consulting a medium. Sometimes if the mourner comes too soon, his or her loved one does not have the strength to come through directly. Often a relative, such as a grandparent, will accompany them to the séance room. When the deceased relative does come though, the spirit will comment, "I knew I was dead because I no longer was in pain," or "I saw my mother and father who greeted me."

Many times, spirit is more at peace than those they left behind. So much so, the newly deceased consider the day of their death as their heavenly birthday. Spiritualists like to acknowledge this date by placing flowers or saying a prayer for the deceased. In any case, it is important to find a way to memorialize the deceased. Sometimes this devotion may be rewarded by a dream visitation or even an unexpected gift, such as finding a penny or spotting a hummingbird or butterfly. Why are these items significant? A penny with "In God we trust" on its face represents faith. In shamanic lore, a hummingbird, which can fly long distances, is considered to be the messenger between the two worlds. In the West, the butterfly, which emerges from its early cocoon in magnificent color, represents a successful transition to the afterlife.

Once a loved one's death is accepted, there is still much to be done. Sometimes the hardest part of grieving is learning what to do with all the love that was shared in life. Men are more likely to move on, while women often experience prolonged grief. For example, John Gunther chose to adopt a son, Nicholas, with his second wife, Jane. Frances Gunther, on the other hand, never remarried or had another child. A devout Zionist, she moved to Israel to help build the Jewish community.

A more recent example of building community came out of the December 14, 2012, school shooting in Sandy Hook, Connecticut. Volunteers deeply touched by the loss of twenty-six of the state's citizens built twenty-six playgrounds to honor the victims. It seemed a fitting tribute, since twenty of the victims were children gunned down that morning.

Often parents choose to honor their deceased child by giving a scholarship in their child's name. When Leland Stanford and his wife, Jane, lost their sixteen-year-old son to typhoid fever in 1884, they decided that "the children of California would be our children."[6] They immortalized Leland Stanford Jr. by setting up a school in his name—Stanford University. The school, which opened its doors on October 1, 1891, continues to expand, including the addition of Stanford Research Institute (SRI) in 1946.

In 1972, SRI physicists Harold E. Puthoff and Russell Targ investigated psychic phenomena as part of a program funded by the CIA for remote viewing. They worked with Uri Geller, the most celebrated psychic of the day. In the early 1970s they tested his ability to bend spoons and other objects.[7] Recently, Uri Geller stated that there is more power in positive thinking than predicting colors on cards. He urges people to use positive thinking and gratitude to overcome life's challenges.[8]

Perhaps the only positive aspect to death is that the loved one is no longer suffering. Though family and friends miss him or her, they still exist, but on a higher plane. As part of the healing process, take time to make a gratitude list to remember all the positive attributes of the deceased and the relationship. Remember: "Tis better to have loved and lost than never to have loved at all."[9]

Write Your Own Obituary Exercise

Writing your own obituary can be a life-affirming experience. It is a way to figure out not only how you wish to be remembered, but how you wish to live your life. You may either write in the first person or third person. It is up to you.

In any event, start at the end point of the obituary and list your life's accomplishments. How do you wish to be remembered? Take a moment and consider your most important achievement.

Now you are ready to list the facts of your life. Begin with your full name, followed by birth date and age, and date and cause of death. List your loved ones: partners, children, long-time friends, and even pets. Usually those who precede you in death are listed first, and then your surviving family and friends.

Next, add your resume details: education and work, degrees, and military service. You may wish to include any notable achievements or honors at this point. This can be followed by civic or church organizations. Take time to add special interests and hobbies.

Finally, you need to give the date, time, and place of your funeral or wake. Be sure to specify if it is a public or private event. When you are finished, read it over. Is there anything else you would like to add? Perhaps you would like to put in a favorite quote or family story.

CHAPTER FOURTEEN

The Only Cure is a Soul Cure

All healing comes from wisdom, faith spiritual knowledge, and God.
—Olga Worhall

Dreams, meditation, and mediums all can be sources of healing. However, there is more to a cure than people realize. Unless the source of illness is detected, the healer can only alleviate symptoms. As Rev. Gladys Custance, a Spiritualist medium of more than fifty years, explained, "The only real cure is a soul cure." Never one to mince words, Mrs. Custance advised students to hold fast to the truth. She kept

Reverend Kenneth Custance
and Reverend Gladys Custance.
Author's collection.

her regular doctors' appointments, as well as her sessions with spirit. She maintained a list of people in dire straits who required daily prayer. She also took time to sit in silence and meditate over the list, sending affirmations of health and strength out. Whenever possible, those who needed healing would attend her weekly healing service at the First Spiritualist Church of Onset, Massachusetts. She made a point to add the names of the sick to the prayer list on the altar.

Mrs. Custance, who suffered from asthma, was a great believer in faith healing. Once, she and her husband, Rev. Kenneth Custance, spent time in England in the company of Harry Edwards. When she mentioned that her asthma was making it hard for her to give the service the next morning, the famous Spiritualist healer told her not to worry. That night at 10:00 p.m., which was his time for healing, Mrs. Custance felt waves of energy hitting her chest. She felt well enough to go to sleep and in the morning made it to the church service.

There are many fine faith healers in addition to those of the Spiritualist faith. Two prominent ones come to mind—Ambrose and Olga Worhall. Both Worhalls were quite psychic. Olga remembers seeing dead people when she was about three. It became a source of concern when Ambrose Worhall, a fellow college student, asked for her hand in marriage. She answered him by saying, "Oh you don't want to marry me. I see dead people." "Never mind," he said, "so do I."[1]

Even in the beginning of their relationship, unusual things would occur. For instance, when Ambrose took a picture of his wife, dead people would frequently show up in the photograph.[2] The Baltimore engineer took it all in stride. In addition to his technical skill, he was a gifted healer who lectured widely on ESP and spiritual healing at colleges and church groups. In 1961, he wrote *The Gift of Healing*. Later on he coauthored *Basic Principles of Spiritual Healing* with Olga.

After her husband's death on February 2, 1972, Olga continued to hold healing services every Thursday morning at the Mount Washington Methodist Church in Baltimore. She was encouraged by the thousands of letters from people who had been healed—including praise from Dr. Bernie Siegel. Not too sure about faith healing, Dr. Siegel had to be pushed forward for a healing session, offered at the American Holistic Medical Association conference. Olga Worhall sat him down and placed her hand on his leg, which had been injured training for a marathon. According to the author of *Man, Medicine, and Miracles*, "The heat from her hands was incredible. I remember putting my hands on the opposite leg to compare the heat sensation. There was no sense of warmth from my hands coming through the dungarees."[3] Much to his chagrin, the pain in his leg was gone and he could walk as usual.

How could this have happened? Ambrose Worhall, ever the engineer, would have explained, "The spiritual healer must be more than a simple conductor; he must function like a complex electronic circuit, because the healing current appears to have, among other things, qualities akin to voltage, frequency, and wavelength."[4] Olga Worhall, on the other hand, believed that "Spiritual healing is the art of restoring a person (or other living entity) to a condition of health by the use of powers usually attributed to the Supreme Being and various saints."[5]

One cannot help but wonder why the Supreme Being restores some people to health and not others. In the West, doctors examine psychological issues. For example, many injured workers are reluctant to return to a job they do not like—especially if they receive payments in the form of unemployment or workers' compensation. Psychologists term this "secondary gain."

However, even if an individual sincerely desires to be well, there may other factors at play. In the East, spiritual counselors talk about karmic conditions from past lives. There are three types of karma:

1. **Sanchita or "piled-up" karma:** the entire debt and credit from all past lives
2. **Prarabdha or "beginning" karma:** The portion assigned in the current life—sometimes termed destiny. Hindu astrologers ascertain this karma through the horoscope.
3. **Kriyamana karma:** actions in this current life that will affect future incarnation

Illnesses that are the result of actions in the current life are often easily resolved. For instance, a smoker with a bad cough may choose to stop smoking. This positive action will bring better health. However, if the condition is due to past-life karma, it may require more effort, but the cough can still be cured both by a change of habit and a change of attitude. Many smokers neglect to work on themselves and may give up smoking or turn to food for relief of tension, thereby creating another health problem.

If an illness is due to a severe karmic condition, or sanchita, it may take many years or even lifetimes to resolve. Such was the case for Thomas Sugrue, a close friend of Edgar Cayce's son Hugh Lynn. In 1926, Hugh Lynn met Thomas Sugrue at Washington and Lee University. A devout Catholic, Sugrue was skeptical about reincarnation. Eventually, he changed his mind and received a total of seventy-six readings from the Sleeping Prophet. He was told that he had been a scribe in ancient Egypt. "Tom's most relevant incarnation was as a scribe in ancient Egypt when he had become involved in a conspiracy that pitted Edgar Cayce, then the high priest Ra Ta, against Hugh Lynn, who was the Pharaoh."[6]

This set the stage for karma in the present. Ironically, Sugrue, who helped build the hospital at Virginia Beach for the Cayce treatments, spent his last years in a wheelchair. After he was taken ill from a rare form of arthritis, he moved to Virginia Beach in June 1939 to live with the Cayce family. While Sugrue did not receive a complete healing, he did receive much encouragement from the readings, which advised a special diet, injections of medication, a pure lifestyle, and release of worry, "for worry will bring the greater disturbances for the system."[7]

Thomas Sugrue took the psychic's advice to heart and made the best of his opportunities in this life. He chose to focus on his talent as a scribe and not his illness, which persisted despite medical treatment and sincere spiritual effort. His positive attitude made it possible to write a biography of Edgar Cayce, which he completed just before his death at age forty-five in 1941. *There Is a River*, published in 1943, made Cayce famous.

Those who suffer from chronic illness, such as Thomas Sugrue, often pray for a soul cure. Perhaps no prayer has received more attention than the Serenity Prayer—the prayer of Saint Francis of Assisi, adopted by Alcoholics Anonymous. Millions use the prayer in the throes of temptation, despair, or illness. Those who believe in a Higher Power know the only true healing is a soul healing.

God grant me the serenity to accept the things I cannot change, courage to change the things I can, and wisdom to know the difference.

CHAPTER FIFTEEN

Good Health– Accept No Substitute

See no evil, hear no evil, speak no evil.

—Ancient proverb

Sometimes, surrender to a higher power is the first step to perfect health. Despondent after a divorce, which took her from the lap of luxury to near poverty, Ann Wigmore turned to the Bible for inspiration. When she came to Daniel 4:333, she stopped at the biblical story of King Nebuchadnezzar. These words stood out: "He was driven from men and did eat grass as oxen, and his body was wet with the dew of heaven, till his hairs were grown like eagles' feathers, and his nails like birds' claws."

As she tuned into the phrase, Wigmore focused on the words "eating grass." It brought her back to her childhood in Lithuania, where she helped her grandmother prepare natural remedies. Surely this was a sign that grass could be healing. Wasn't that what dogs did when they were ill? That is when she started experimenting with wheatgrass. In the 1940s, the intuitive nutritionist used wheatgrass and raw vegetables as a means of detoxing the body. "She believed that fresh wheatgrass juice and fresh vegetables—and especially chlorophyll—retained more of their original energy and potency (a form of vitalism) if they were uncooked and eaten as soon as possible after harvesting them."[1]

In 1961, she and fellow Lithuanian Viktoras Kulvinskas opened the Hippocrates Health Institute at 25 Exeter Street—the elegant brownstone of Boston brahim Margaret Drumheller. She and Viktoras gave weekly Sunday open-house events. Those who attended came from all walks of life: college students interested in nutrition, others who simply wished to improve their overall health, along with those diagnosed with terminal illnesses, and the residents who lived at the institute.

She knew it was not easy to rebuild health, but her compassion for the ill was boundless. She often took time to talk to residents daily with her pet monkey,

Elwood Babbitt.
Courtesy of Daria Babbitt.

Precious, at her side. On Sunday, she had a weekly potluck supper to introduce people to her diet. She believed that "Simple, uncooked foods such as fresh vegetables, greens, fruits, sprouted seeds, grains, beans, and nuts, along with pure liquids, such as fresh vegetable juices, fruit juices, and 'green drinks' made from a variety of sprouts, greens, and vegetables, are nutritious yet light on digestion."[2] This beloved lady remained active in the Hippocrates Health Institute in West Palm Beach, Florida, until her death in 1994.

While Ann Wigmore believed in wheatgrass, Marcia Moore turned to yoga for perfect health. She was born to a wealthy family: her father, Robert L. Moore, was the founder of the Sheridan Hotel chain. She was introduced to Eastern thought by her mother, Eleanor Moore, who was an ardent theosophist. In 1955, Marcia, along with her husband, Simon Roof, and their three children, took an extended trip to India, where they studied Eastern religions. After her graduation from Radcliffe College, she began teaching yoga in her Concord home.

In 1965, the Boston-area yoga instructor became famous through Jess Stearn's book *Yoga, Youth and Reincarnation*. The book chronicles the author's attempt to regain youthful vitality through yoga—not an easy task for the middle-aged New Yorker. For instance, when Marcia tried teaching the Sun poses, which she called Suryanamaskar, Stearn balked at the twelve positions. He quipped, "How do I do an exercise when I can't even remember it?"[3] She then taught him less complicated exercises: the Plough, Locus, Cobra, and Bow. Marcia smiled at his efforts, noting her student's "subconscious wants the body to give up so it can get on with its routine aging process." However, Jess Stearn did not give up. He followed a yoga regimen of exercises, which he details in photo and outline form at the back of his book. After three months of hatha yoga, going to bed early, eating a healthful diet, and meditating, Stearn regained his youthful physique and vigor![4]

By the way, Marcia Moore advocated a vegetarian diet. After *Yoga, Youth, and Reincarnation* was published, she wrote a book of her own—*Yoga, Science of the Self*—which she coauthored with her second husband, Mark Douglas. As her fame grew, she attracted a following of celebrities to her Ojai California, residence. By the time of her death in 1979, she was living in the Seattle area with her new husband, Howard Alltounian, MD. Sadly, Moore mysteriously disappeared in 1979. When her remains were discovered two years later, many believed that she had been murdered; others felt she had walked into the night and, in an altered state, fallen to her death. The fact remains that Marcia Moore died at age fifty, much too young. This gifted and well-educated writer left behind a legacy of yoga, astrology, and reincarnation texts.

One of last avenues that Marcia Moore was exploring was that of metaphysics, which she tried to access through hallucinogenic drugs. Others, such as Elwood Babbitt, have the ability to reach the higher worlds thought the time-honored method of channeling. Even as a teenager, he had experiences of mediumship. His main spirit guide was Dr. Fischer, who acted as a gatekeeper to keep out unwanted spirits. By 1978, Babbitt became a well-known channeler after the release of his biography, *Voices in Spirit*, written by Professor Charles Hapgood.

A few years before his death in 2001, Elwood Babbitt channeled his last book, *Perfect Health: Accept No Substitutes*. The book includes spirit communications from the spirits of Edgar Cayce, Dr. Fischer, Dr. Fu Man Lu, Albert Einstein, and Dr. Royal Rife, an American contemporary of Wilhelm Reich. While many of their spirit retain views that they held when they were on earth, some, such as the late Edgar Cayce, wish to update their work. For example, in the 1930s he stated that 1998 would bring a pole shift and vast earth changes. Cayce explained that this prophecy did not come true. "Some of my prophecies, of course, did not work as they should have according to time, but I regret to say the conditioning of time, the free will of through forces of the collective individuals can change the set destiny I would have seen at that time.[5] Apparently free will played a role in delaying events.

While Edgar Cayce is well known, few know the name of Dr. Royal Rife. He discovered a cure for cancer in the 1930s, when he invented a "frequency treatment" machine for "Mortal Oscillatory Rate" to destroy organisms by vibrating them at this particular rate. According to author Barry Lynes's book *The Rife Report*, within a three-minute period, his machine could painlessly destroy viruses or bacteria without damage to tissue.[6] Sadly, Rife was put in jail and all his papers were destroyed. It is comforting to note that Dr. Rife is still practicing medicine on the Other Side of life, where he is now an advocate of nature as a means to improve health.

Elwood Babbitt was a great admirer of another revolutionary physician, Wilhelm Reich, the Austrian psychiatrist who attributed diseases to emotional blocks. While today's psychologists are beginning to understand the mind-body connection, in the 1930s and 1940s this idea was unconventional, and many considered the idea of orgone or life energy to be ridiculous. Eventually, Reich was imprisoned in Lewisburg, Pennsylvania, where he died in 1957.

Apparently, Dr. Reich still dispenses advice from the Other Side of life. When one man asked about depression, the doctor explained that the depression emanated from his "own fears and uncertainties of life, from those intimately associated with your life as well as the thought pollutions that surround you."[7] Evidently, depression stems as much from inner anxiety as well as a toxic emotional environment.

How then to achieve good health? Ann Wigmore advocated ridding the body of toxins with wheatgrass and a raw-food diet. Marcia Moore turned to yoga, and Elwood Babbitt sought advice from the spirit side of life. Perhaps perfect health requires all three: a balanced body, an even mind, and a positive spirit. One thing is for sure: when it comes to good health, accept no substitute!

What Do the Doctors Say?

What drains your spirit drains your body.

—Silver Birch

Good health is the goal both of the spiritual healer and traditional physician. At a glance, the two groups seem worlds apart; however, some medical doctors have managed to bridge this gap. Seven come to mind: Dr. Harold Reilly, Dr. Norman Shealy, Dr. Douglas Baker, Dr. Leon Curry, Dr. Deloris Krieger, Dr. Judith Orloff, and Dr. Mona Lisa Schultz. Each has examined spiritual healing with good results.

In the 1930s, Dr. Reilly first became acquainted with Edgar Cayce when Cayce began sending referrals. At the time, Reilly had an office in Rockefeller Center in New York. Many famous patients such as Sonja Henie, Gloria Swanson, Mae West, Gypsy Rose Lee, Leslie Caron, Joan Fontaine, Nelson Rockefeller, Jess Stearn, and Bob Hope came for his physical therapy. Comedian Bob Hope quipped, "After the fine conditioning of Harold J. for eighteen years, I feel that everyone should live the life of Reilly."[1]

Reilly naturally assumed that Edgar Cayce was a doctor. He was quite surprised to find that "Doctor Cayce" was actually a trance medium. Eventually, Reilly had several readings with Cayce, which he termed "miraculous."[2] While worlds apart in education, Reilly and Cayce were on the same page in regard to healing. Both believed that a healthy body can heal itself given the right nutrients, exercise, and relaxation. The physiotherapist advocated a nutritious diet, with good assimilation of nutriments, proper elimination, and good circulation to maintain health. According to Dr. Reilly, "The Cayce 'readings' and the Reilly therapy aim at producing a healthy body that will heal itself of the ailment."[3] He gave many examples of natural cures in his book *The Edgar Cayce Handbook for Health through Drugless Therapy*.

Dr. Norman Shealy did not have the privilege that Reilly had of a personal relationship with Edgar Cayce, but Shealy was just as enthusiastic as Reilly. When the graduate of Duke University School of Medicine was introduced to the Cayce material in 1972, it changed the doctor's life. He credits Cayce with having laid the

Harold J. Reilly (1895–1987). *Courtesy of the Association for Research and Enlightenment.*

foundation for holistic medicine. Inspired by Cayce, Dr. Shealy founded the American Holistic Medical Association in 1978. Since then he has written several books that embrace the Cayce philosophy, including *Medial Intuition, Energy Medicine,* and *Blueprint for Healing.*[4]

One of Shealy's coauthors, Caroline Myss, put it most succinctly: "What drains your spirit drains your body." Myss began doing medical intuitive readings for Dr. Shealy in 1984. Her high degree of accuracy inspired him, and the two wrote *The Creation of Health: The Emotional, Psychological, and Spiritual Responses That Promote Health and Healing,* which came out in 1987. Ten years later, Myss wrote her own book, *Anatomy of the Spirit,* which became a classic in the field of energy medicine. Myss now divides her time between writing and doing workshops on the spiritual and psychological roadblocks to health. In 2003, she founded the Caroline Myss Educational Institute (CMED) in Chicago, Illinois, to teach others how to become skilled practitioners.[5]

In addition to studying Edgar Cayce, doctors such as Douglas Baker have also been drawn to theosophy. Dr. Baker was born in England and immigrated to South Africa, where he volunteered in the Natel Mounted Rifles at age sixteen. During the war, he became aware of "the powers latent in man." After the war he began extensive studies in esoteric astrology and psychology, alternative methods of healing, complementary medicine, yoga, and meditation. He joined the Theosophical Society and the Swedenborg Society. Eventually, he became a doctor and medical advisor to the De La Warr Laboratories in Oxford, where he researched the effects of biomagnetism on the human aura. In the 1970s, Dr. Baker established Claregate College, a correspondence school.

Dr. Baker views illness both from a medical and metaphysical viewpoint of a clairvoyant whose guide is Master Robert Browning. For example, Baker feels that arthritis is due to an inflexible attitude in this life and perhaps a past life as well. According to Baker, the author of *Esoteric Healing,* "The arthritis imposes such a burden of effort on the patient that he inevitably longs to be free [from his rigidity]. This is helpful to the soul, and in the lives ahead concretized attitudes in the personality vehicle become undermined, and freer expression of the soul results."[6] As for treatment, the doctor recommends counseling on the karma nature along with a positive attitude, natural herbs, and magnesium supplements.[7] More information is available in his books, and videos which can be viewed at www.claregategroup. org/index.php/videos1/douglas-baker-videos.

Dr. Douglas Baker, by the way, is not the only theosophist to make an impact on healing. Another theosophist, clairvoyant Dora Kunz, teamed with Dr. Dolores Krieger to develop Therapeutic Touch. In this noncontact form of healing, practitioners of therapeutic touch/place their hands over a patient to send energy to the patient's energy field. They are encouraged to tune into the area that needs healing by scanning with their hand. Then they project colored energy to the afflicted area. For instance, a Therapeutic Touch (TT) practitioner would send healing green light to a place of inflammation. By 2006, Therapeutic Touch was being taught in eighty colleges and universities spread over seventy countries, as well as in some eighty hospitals in North America where it is practiced.[8]

While Delores Krieger did much to organize this form of spiritual healing, it was Dora Kunz who discovered the healing powers of touch. She had a most unusual upbringing. Her father owned a sugarcane plantation in the Dutch East Indies; her mother was a believer in clairvoyance. Both her parents had been members of the Theosophical Society. From an early age, Dora interacted with ethereal beings. At eleven years old she moved to Sydney, Australia, to study psychic C. W. Leadbeater. Her 1927 marriage to American educator and writer Fritz Kunz brought her to the New York City area.

Dora Kunz became well known in theosophical circles for her ability to see the human aura and describe its properties. She began to philanthropically assist physicians with complicated medical cases, and she was able to view the aura of the patients. "More specifically, she reported the existence of centers of energy in the human body, also known as chakras, changing their colors according to diseases that affect matching endocrine glands."[9] Kunz was familiar with ancient yogic techniques of pranic healing methods that transfer energy from one person to another. She also continued to be active in theosophy. After her husband's death in 1971, Dora moved to Wheaton, Illinois, when she was elected president of the Theosophical Society in America in 1975. In 1989, she wrote *The Chakras and the Human Energy Fields*, coauthored with Dr. Shafica Karagulla. This work was followed by *The Personal Aura* (1991) and *Spiritual Healing* (1995).

Dora Kunz was a natural clairvoyant. However, not everyone who is a medical clairvoyant is born with the ability. Some, such as noted medical intuitive Greta Alexander, acquired the gift as an adult. In a 1990 interview, Greta explained how her psychic sense opened after she was struck by lightning. At the time, she was pregnant with her fifth child. Fortunately, neither she nor the baby was harmed.[10] Soon after the birth of her new daughter, the housewife from rural Illinois became known for her unusual psychic abilities.

When a college friend told Dr. Leon Curry in 1975 about a psychic who could find missing people and diagnose illnesses, he was skeptical. On a dare, he called Greta. "What do you have to do with airplanes?" she asked. His surprised answer: "I just climbed out of one."[11] Eventually, the two met and began working together. Dr. Curry would send the medical intuitive handprints of patients for her to examine.

"Time and time again, Greta could look at a patient's handprint and tell Dr. Curry about that patient's esophagus, or liver, or lungs—even when the patient was seven states away." Dr. Curry gives many case histories in his book, *The Doctor and the Psychic*. Sometimes Greta Alexander even mentioned illnesses that had not yet been diagnosed.[12]

In the 1970s, medical clairvoyants were relatively unknown. However, in more-recent years, largely due to the efforts of two medical doctors, Dr. Judith Orloff and Dr. Mona Lisa Schulz, the phenomenon is more accepted. Dr. Orloff, the daughter of two physicians, grew up in Beverly Hills. Even as a child, she had intuitive experiences, since she was a natural empath. In 1996, the board-certified psychiatrist wrote her first book, *Second Sight*, in which she describes her own second sight and the use of energy psychiatry in psychotherapy. In 2009, she published *Emotional Freedom*, in which she synthesized neuroscience, intuitive medicine, psychology, and subtle-energy techniques.

Dr. Mona Lisa Schultz is also one of the rare physicians who can combine intuition, science, medicine, and mysticism. The board-certified psychiatrist has been a medical intuitive for over thirty years and is the coauthor of *All Is Well*. The book separates the body into seven groups of emotional centers. Dr. Schultz, along with Louise Hay, also describes common mental causes for physical illness. Their book includes advice on traditional and alternative medicine, affirmations, and nutrition.

Later, Dr. Schultz penned *The Intuitive Advisor* to assist people who are emotionally trapped in unhappy relationships, family troubles, or dead-end jobs. Dr. Schultz also gives medical intuitive consultations, which are done over the phone. According to her website, she requires only your name and age in order to describe the condition of your physical body. The psychic physician will also give "detailed solutions on how to rewire the emotional patterns that she sees aggravate your health, and then she will begin the process of teaching you how to change those thought patterns. In addition, she will 'educate' you on the array of solutions available to ease the physical symptoms of your health problem including nutritional supplements, herbs, medicines, physical remedies like EMDR, neuro-muscular therapy, and others."[13]

Both Dr. Schulz and Dr. Orloff can diagnose and prescribe because they are licensed physicians. On the other hand, the majority of medical intuitives, such as Greta Alexander, work in conjunction with licensed professionals. While this practice is best for the patient, too-few physicians are willing to consider even the possibility of medical intuitives. This is unlikely to change until there is a shift in consciousness. As more medical experts examine the benefits of alternative modalities, such as acupuncture, herbal remedies, and shamanic practices, they may also consider the benefits of clairvoyance. When that day arrives, the ancient wisdom is likely to become the new paradigm.

Epilogue

Recently, I was going through my files and came upon notes from a reading given by Dr. Douglas Baker in 1971. That spring, Baker was promoting his soon-to-be-opened Claregate College, which offered courses in the esoteric sciences. At the time I attended the English clairvoyant's lectures, I was studying to be to become a Spiritualist healer and was keen to learn more about medical clairvoyance.

I was so impressed with Baker's lectures on karma, reincarnation, and clairvoyance that I had a private reading with him. The doctor not only correctly diagnosed my anemia but recommended radionics as a treatment or, if preferred, the traditional iron tablets. He also took time to discuss and diagram the rays of the body. According to theosophy, everyone has seven bodies—each of which is associated with a different ray. At the end of the session, he told me, "You may not be ready for this material for twenty-five to thirty years from now."

I realized that just a little over thirty years had passed, and so much had happened after that evidential reading. The next year (1972), I became a certified medium in May, married my husband, Ronald, in November, and moved to Connecticut. My own clairvoyance developed to the point where I too saw auras and gave readings. On occasion, I have also had glimpses of the Ascended Master Moyra. After typing the notes from Dr. Baker's reading, I realized that the masters are always a step ahead of us.

My love of learning has continued unabated. I have made it a point to attend lectures at Kripalu Holistic Institute in Lennox, Massachusetts, whenever the spirit moves me. I have taken workshops with Dr. Alberto Villodo, James van Praagh, Caroline Myss, Dr. Mona Lisa Schulz, and Karen Grace Kassey. They all are insightful speakers who have been an inspiration to me.

However, the most incredible healing that I experienced was still that of psychic surgeon Alex Orbito. Today, when I show students the film of Orbito doing psychic surgery, I say, "I know it is real and I can tell you how he does it." It is not Orbito, but spirit entities that perform the surgery. When he is in trance, his spirit guide incorporates and uses Orbito's hands to operate on the patient. These entities of light can literally interpenetrate matter.

Since my psychic surgery in 1993, I have witnessed countless healings performed by John of God, the Brazilian healer who also does psychic surgery. John of God guides have removed tumors, corrected eyesight, and even restored flesh damaged beyond medical repair. One of the most poignant examples of this is Bob Dinga. In 1986, he was diagnosed with a rare retina disorder. In a period of fifteen years, he had five laser surgeries. Still, he was legally blind. His doctors could do no more than to advise their patient to learn Braille.

In 1998, his partner, Diana, gave him a copy of Robert Pellegrino-Estrich's book *The Miracle Man*. After reading the story of John of God, Dinga decided to visit Casa de Dom Inácio in Brazil. It took several trips to John of God, but eventually his eyesight began to improve significantly. Today, Bob Dinga leads a normal life again and even takes tours to visit John of God in Brazil.

It is not always necessary to have a psychic surgery. Some people have what is called "invisible surgery" in which there is no physical contact with John of God. He simply prays over the group, and the entities do invisible healings. Such was the case for my friend Mary. She came with my husband, Ron, and me on our trip to Brazil in 2007. Mary, an RN, had asthma so severe that she almost died from an attack at age twenty-one. When she returned from Brazil, she visited her specialist. The doctor was surprised to find no traces of asthma. He asked, "What have you been doing, Mary?" When she told the doctor, "I went to see John of God in Brazil for healing," he shook his head in disbelief.

It is hard to believe that spirits can heal by their presence; however, they were all around us at the Casa. Even the smallest care seemed to concern them. For instance, on the first day, when I had difficulty getting money from the ATM in Anápolis, the spirit of Saint Rita appeared to apologize for not being able to help with the banking. As she sat on the bed next to me, she explained, "Your world has its rules, and our world has its own." I was so thrilled by the visitation that I quickly let go of any disappointment.

I have seen many spirit guides around John of God, including Jesus. When I volunteered in 2014 at Omega for three days, I was about ten feet from John of God during the healings. My job was to direct people to the correct line and to make sure everyone kept their eyes shut during the healing sessions. At one point, I looked out on the crowd, sitting in meditation, and saw Jesus in a white robe walking in the back. He gently touched each person as he walked between the aisles, starting from the back. When I asked Heather Cumming, John of God's translator, which spirit had incorporated in the medium's body that morning, she said that it was that of Saint Francis of Xavier. Then she added, "Jesus often comes when Saint Francis of Xavier is present."

ENDNOTES

Chapter One: HOLY MEDICINE

1. http://ancientegyptonline.co.uk/sekhmet.html.
2. www.metmuseum.org/toah/hd/egam/hd_egam.htm.
3. www.historywiz.com/didyouknow/asclepius.html.
4. www.alchemylab.com/daimon.htm.
5. Hippocrates of Cos (1923). "The Oath," Loeb Classical Library. 147: 298–299. doi:10.4159/DLCL.hippocrates_cos-oath.1923.
6. www.drweil.com/health-wellness/balanced-living/wellness-therapies/ayurvedic-medicine.
7. Jon Klimo, *Channeling* (Berkeley, CA: North Atlantic Books, 1998), 107.
8 Rosemary Guiley, *Harper's Encyclopedia of Mystical and Paranormal Experience* (San Francisco: Harper, 1991), 329–330.
9. Holy Bible, Matthew 4:23–24.
10. www.centuryone.com/25dssfacts.html.
11. http://digilander.libero.it/raxdi/inglese/miraf.htm.
12. Rosemary Guiley, *Harper's Encyclopedia of Mystical and Paranormal Experience* (San Francisco: Harper, 1991), 426.
13. www.meilach.com/spiritual/misc/other.html.
14. Andrew Jackson David, *The Magic Staff* (Boston, MA: William White & Company), 263.
15. www.andrewjacksondavis.com.
16. Ibid.
17. Edgar Cayce, Reading 1472–2.

Chapter Two: ESOTERIC ANATOMY

1. www.pbs.org/wgbh/nova/body/hippocratic-oath-today.html.
2. www.oprah.com/omagazine/extraordinary-knowing-by-elizabeth-lloyd-mayer-book-review#ixzz4bb4PBkdD.
3. Serge Kahili King, *Serge King Earth Energies: A Quest for the Hidden Power of the Planet*, 1992, Chapter 3 The Odic Force and Reichenbach, pp. 38–604.
4. Ibid.
5. Ibid.
6. *An Appreciation of C. W. Leadbeater* by Geoffrey Hodson.
7. www.anandgholap.net/Dreams-CWL.htm.
8. www.anandgholap.net/Dreams-CWL.htm.
9. www.amazon.com/Esoteric-Healing-Part-3 ebook.
10. Dr. Douglas Baker, *The Seven Pillars of Ancient Wisdom*, Vol. 3, Part 2, *Esoteric Healing* (Essendon, UK: Little Elephant, 1976).
11. Ibid.

12. www.rosalynlbruyere.org.
13. www.barbarabrennan.com/welcome/healing_science.html.

Chapter Three: DEVELOPING INTUITION

1. Joseph McMoneagle, *The Stargate Chronicles: Memoirs of a Psychic Spy; The Remarkable Life of U.S. Government Remote Viewer 001* (Kindle, Location 1024). Crossroad Press, Kindle Edition.
2. Joseph McMoneagle, *The Stargate Chronicles: Memoirs of a Psychic Spy; The Remarkable Life of U.S. Government Remote Viewer 001* (Kindle, Locations 1097–1101). Crossroad Press, Kindle Edition.
3. https://jhaines6.wordpress.com/2011/04/19/jung-in-conversation-with-a-native-american-chief.
4. Edgar Cayce, Reading 1861–19.
5. http://zestinfusion.com.au/mindfulness-meditation.

Chapter Four: DEVELOPING CLAIRVOYANCE

1. *Coast to Coast with George Noory*, radio program, January 30, 2017.
2. Henry Steel Olcutt, *Old Diary Leaves* (Madras, India: C. P. Putnam and Sons, 1895).
3. www.intuitiveheart.com/texts/visionary.
4. Joseph H. Merrill, *Healing* (Indianapolis, IN: Summit, 1979), 26–27.
5. P. H. Abelson, (21 June 1974). "Pseudoscience". Science. 184 (4143): 1233–1233. doi:10.1126/science.184.4143.1233.
6. *An Appreciation of C. W. Leadbeater* by Geoffrey Hodson.

Chapter Five: READING THE AURA

1. Edgar Cayce, *Auras* (Virginia Beach, VA: ARE Press, 1973), 17.
2. Edgar Cayce, *Auras* (Virginia Beach, VA: ARE Press, 1973), 18.
3. Tina Zion, *Become a Medical Intuitive* (San Francisco: WriteLife, 2015).

Chapter Six: SPIRIT GUIDES

1. www.angelfire.com/ok/SilverBirch/divine.html.
2. Ibid.
3. Frederick Harding, "Why American Indians Are Spirit Guides?" (Lily Dale, NY: Stowe Memorial Foundation, 1940), 5.
4. King, D. Brett (2009). The Roman Period and the Middle Ages. In D. B. King, Viney, W. D. Woody (Eds.) *A History of Psychology: Ideas and Context*, 4th ed., pp. 70–71 (Boston, Massachusetts: Pearson Education, Inc.).
5. Slater Brown, *The Heyday of Spiritualism* (New York: Pocket Books Edition, 1972), 90.
6. Ibid., 91.
7. Ibid., 93–94.
8. Andrew Jackson Davis, *Principles of Nature* (New York: S. S. Lyon and William Fishbough, 1847), 62.

9. Thomas Sugrue, (1942). *There Is a River.* (Virginia Beach, VA: ARE Press (50th Anniversary edition), p. 118.

10. Gina Cerminara, "The Medical Clairvoyance of Edgar Cayce," in *Many Mansions* (New York: New American Library, 1999), 14.

11. Thomas Sugrue, *There Is a River* (Virginia Beach, CA: ARE Press, 2003), 290–300.

12. www.theosophical.org/publications/quest-magazine/3603.

13. www3.telus.net/st_simons/cr9801.htm.

14. http://psychics.co.uk/blog/famous-spiritual-healers.

15. www.johnofgod-brazil.net/john-of-god/who-is-john-of-god.

16. www.johnofgod-brazil.net/john-of-god/the-healing-process.

17. www.azquotes.com/quote/1460993.

Chapter Seven: HEALING ANGELS

1. www.edgarcayce.org/about-us/blog/blog-posts/the-little-prophetess-from-the-cayce-readings

2. Ibid.

3. "Geoffrey Hodson Story," Theosophical Order of Service New Zealand.

4. Geoffrey Hodson, *The Brotherhood of Angels and Man* (Wheaton, IL: Theosophical Publishing, 1982), 82.

5. www.angelspeake.com/about.html.

6. www.lasplash.com/publish/cat_index_art_and_books/psychic-kim-o-neil-interview.phpe.

7. www.bookpeople.com/event/kim-oneill-way-know.

Chapter Eight: CLEARING NEGATIVE SPIRITS

1. Dr. Carl Wickland, *Thirty Years among the Dead* (Kindle, Locations 15033–15043). Rev. Steven Earl York, Kindle Edition.

2. Ibid.

3. Dr. Edith Fiore, *The Unquiet Dead* (New York: Ballantine Books, 1995), 78.

4. Dr. Alberto Villoldo told this antidote at Omega Institute workshop.

Chapter Nine: HANDS-ON HEALING

1. http://riotimesonline.com/brazil-news/rio-travel/finding-the-spiritist-movement-in-brazil.

2. John G. Fuller, *ARIGO: Surgeon of the Rusty Knife* (Kindle, Locations 240–242). BookBaby, Kindle Edition, 240 of 3540.

3. John G. Fuller, ARIGO: *Surgeon of the Rusty Knife* (Kindle, Locations 246–248). BookBaby, Kindle Edition.

4. Joe Fisher, (2001). The Siren Call of Hungry Ghosts. Cosimo, Inc. pp. 112–114.

5. http://psychictruth.info/Medium_George_Chapman.htm

6. Bernard Hutton, *Healing Hands*, 2d rev. ed. (London: W. H. Allen, 1978), 64–68.

7. http://psychictruth.info/Medium_George_Chapman.htm.

8. www.spiritualistresources.com/cgi-bin/healing/index.pl?read=5.

9. www.drwaynedyer.com/blog/meeting-spiritual-healer.

10. Ibid.

11. http://emmabragdon.com/brazil-trips.
12. content/uploads/2013/01/spiritist_hospitals_Springer2011.pdf.
13. http://nsac.org/what-we-believe/healing.

Chapter Ten: REMARKABLE HEALINGS
1. www.reiki.org/reikinews/hippocratesB.htm.
2. Holy Bible, John 9–12.
3. www.texasbeyondhistory.net/cabeza-cooking/encounters.html.
4. www.texasbeyondhistory.net/cabeza-cooking/encounters.html.
5. http://phineasquimby.wwwhubs.com.
6. www.ppquimby.com.
7. www.azquotes.com/author/58637-Phineas_Quimby.
8. www.ppquimby.com.
9. Resa Willis, *Mark and Livy: The Love Story of Mark Twain and the Woman Who Almost Tamed Him* (New York and London: Routledge, 2004), 25.
10. www.wrf.org/men-women-medicine/dr-james-newton-healing-gift.php.
11. Dr. J. R. Newton, *The Modern Bethesda* (New York: Newton, 1879), 76.
12. Andrew Jackson Davis, *Principles of Nature* (New York: S. S. Lyon and William Fishbough,1847), 62.
13. www.andrewjacksondavis.com/.
14. W. F. Bynum, *Companion of the Encyclopedia for the History of Medicine*, Google edition, 624.
15. www.healingcancernaturally.com/edgar-cayce-health-healing.html.
16. www.spiritsite.com/writing/edgcay/part5.shtml.
17. www.edgarcayce.org/about-us/reflections/guests/elsie-sechrist.
18. Judith Joslow-Rodewald and Patricia West-Barker, *Healing Spirits* (Freedom, CA: Crossing), 63–64.
19. Ibid.
20. www.amazon.com/Touch-Hope-Dean-Kraft/dp/0399143890/ref=tmm_hrd_swatch_0?_encoding=UTF8&qid=&sr.

Chapter Eleven: AFTERLIFE COMMUNICATIONS
1. www.nytimes.com/2012/11/26/books/dr-eben-alexanders-tells-of-near-death-in-proof-of-heaven.htm.
2. Gary Schwartz, *Afterlife Communication: 16 Proven Methods, 85 True Accounts* (266). Unknown. Kindle Edition.
3. www.articlesnatch.com/Article/Your-Psychic-Psychometry-Powers.
4. J. Gordon Melton (1 September 2007). *The Encyclopedia of Religious Phenomena*. Visible Ink Press. pp. 115, Retrieved 12 May 2013.
5. Larry Dweller, *Beginner's Guide to Mediumship* (York, ME: Weiser Books, 1997), 4.
6. Rosemary Ellen Guiley, *Dreamspeak* (New York: Berkeley Books, 2003), 253.

Chapter Twelve: MEDICAL MEDIUMSHIP

1. Tina M. Zion, *Become a Medical Intuitive: Complete Developmental Course* (Kindle Location 79). Boutique of Quality Book Publishing, Inc. Kindle Edition.
2. Tina M. Zion, *Become a Medical Intuitive: Complete Developmental Course* (Kindle Location 79). Boutique of Quality Book Publishing, Inc. Kindle Edition.
3. www.soundstrue.com/store/science-medical-intuition-course/free-video-series?sq_return_url=http%3A%2F%2Fwww.soundstrue.com%2Fstore%2Fscience-medical-intuition-course.
4. www.goodreads.com/author/quotess/11236.carolinemyss.
5. www.medicalmedium.com-medical-medium-about-anthony-william.
6. Anthony William, *Medical Medium: Secrets Behind Chronic and Mystery Illness and How to Finally Heal* (p. 39). Hay House, Inc. Kindle Edition.
7. Anthony William, *Medical Medium: Secrets Behind Chronic and Mystery Illness and How to Finally Heal* (p. 39). Hay House, Inc. Kindle Edition.
8. Gina Ceminara, "The Medical Clairvoyance of Edgar Cayce," Many Mansions, 1999, p 14.
9. Slater Brown, *The Heyday of Spiritualism*, Mass Market Paperback, p 18.

Chapter Thirteen: HEALING GRIEF

1. John J. Gunther, *Death Be Not Proud* (P. S.) (Kindle, Location 1839). HarperCollins, Kindle Edition.
2. John J. Gunther, *Death Be Not Proud* (P. S.) (Kindle, Locations 2792–2793). HarperCollins, Kindle Edition.
3. www.joycekeller.com/resources/JoPortalFateMag7Pg.pdf.
4. Mark Ireland, *Messages from the Afterlife* (Berkeley CA: North Atlantic Books, 2013), 12–13.
5. www.euro-tongil.org/swedish/english/eford_prologue.htm.
6. www.stanford.edu/about/history.
7. Russell Targ, Harold Puthoff, *Mind-Reach: Scientists Look at Psychic Abilities.* Hampton Roads Publishing Company, 2005.
8. www.coasttocoastam.com/guest/geller-uri/6317.
9. Alfred Lord Tennyson.

Chapter Fourteen: THE ONLY CURE IS A SOUL CURE

1. www.washingtonpost.com/archive/lifestyle/1981/11/07/the-healers-touch/bb8c71dc-faf8-435f-9aa7-d94198f9baa9/?utm_term=.641f7c89feed.
2. www.washingtonpost.com/archive/lifestyle/1981/11/07/the-healers-touch/bb8c71dc-af8-435f-9aa7-d94198f9baa9/?utm_term=.641f7c89feed.
3. http://berniesiegelmd.com/2011/06/consciousness-and-life.
4. https://selfdefinition.org/healing/ambrose-alexander-worrall.htm.
5. https://selfdefinition.org/healing/ambrose-alexander-worrall.htm.
6. Sidney D. Kirkpatrick and Nancy Kirkpatrick, *True Tales from the Edgar Cayce Archives: Lives Touched and Lessons Learned from the Sleeping Prophet* (Kindle, Locations 3000–3001). ARE Press, Kindle Edition.

7. Sidney D. Kirkpatrick and Nancy Kirkpatrick, *True Tales from the Edgar Cayce Archives: Lives Touched and Lessons Learned from the Sleeping Prophet* (Kindle, Locations 3020–3021). ARE Press, Kindle Edition.

Chapter Fifteen: GOOD HEALTH—ACCEPT NO SUBSTITUTE

1. M. Fitzgerald, (2014). *Diet Cults: The Surprising Fallacy at the Core of Nutrition Fads and a Guide to Healthy Eating for the Rest of US.* Pegasus Books. ISBN 978-1-60598-560-2.
2. Ann Wigmore, *Why Suffer?* Healthy Living Publications, Kindle Edition, 149.
3. Jess Stearn, *Yoga, Youth, and Reincarnation* (Virginia Beach, VA: ARE Press, 1997), 53.
4. Ibid., 77.
5. Elwood Babbitt, *Perfect Health: Accept No Substitutes* (Kindle Locations 1941–1946). Light Technology Publishing, Kindle Edition.
6. "Questionable methods of cancer management: electronic devices" (PDF). CA Cancer J. Clin. 44 (2): 115–27. 1994. doi:10.3322/canjclin.44.2.115. PMID 8124604.
7. Elwood Babbitt, *Perfect Health: Accept No Substitutes* (Kindle, Locations 1941–1946). Light Technology Publishing, Kindle Edition.

Chapter Sixteen: WHAT DO THE DOCTORS SAY?

1. Edgar Cayce files, Reading 2696-1 (Source: 3. Harold J. Reilly, *The Edgar Cayce Handbook for Health through Drugless Therapy* (Kindle, Locations 137–140). ARE Press, Kindle Edition.
2. Harold J. Reilly, *The Edgar Cayce Handbook for Health through Drugless Therapy* (Kindle, Locations 291–292). ARE Press, Kindle Edition.
3. Harold J. Reilly, *The Edgar Cayce Handbook for Health through Drugless Therapy* (Kindle, Locations 297–300). ARE Press, Kindle Edition.
4. C. Norman Shealy, *Blueprint for Holistic Healing: Your Practical Guide to Body-Mind-Spirit Health* (Kindle, Locations 169–172). ARE Press, Kindle Edition.
5. C. Norman Shealy, *Blueprint for Holistic Healing: Your Practical Guide to Body-Mind-Spirit Health* (Kindle, Locations 1103–1104). ARE Press, Kindle Edition.
6. Dr. Douglas M. Baker, *Esoteric Healing*, Vol. 1 (Douglas Baker Esoteric Healing Book 1) (Kindle, Locations 522–524). Claregate Ltd., Kindle Edition.
7. Dr. Douglas M. Baker, *Esoteric Healing*, Vol. 1 (Douglas Baker Esoteric Healing Book 1) (Kindle, Locations 548–553). Claregate Ltd., Kindle Edition.
8. www.therapeutictouch.org/what_is_tt.html.
9. Theosophical Publishing House, Dora van Gelder Kunz, Theosophical Society in America, 2010.
10. Interview with Greta Alexander in 1990 by Dr. Leon Curry and Jim Hildebrandt of WTOC-TV.
11 www.facebook.com/The-Doctor-and-The-Psychic-141296332080.
12. http://thedoctorandthepsychic.com.
13. www.drmonalisa.com/private-reading-request.

BIBLIOGRAPHY

Andrews, Ted. *How to See and Read the Aura*. Minneapolis: Llewellyn, 2006.

Babbitt, Elwood. *Perfect Health: Accept No Substitutes*. Flagstaff, AZ: Light Technology, 1993.

Baker, Dr. Douglas M. *Esoteric Healing*. Part 2, *Stress Disorders*. Essendon, UK: Little Elephant, 1976.

Baker, Dr. Douglas M. *Esoteric Healing*. Vol. 1. Llandysul, Wales: Claregate, 1981.

Baumann, Lee T. *Window to God*. CreateSpace, 2010.

Brown, Slater. *The Heyday of Spiritualism*. New York: Pocket Books Edition, 1972.

Bruyere, Rosalyn. *Wheels of Light*. New York: Fireside Book, 1994.

Butler, W. E. *How to Read the Aura*. Rochester, VT: Destiny Books, 1998.

Bynum, W. F. *Companion of the Encyclopedia for the History of Medicine*. Google edition.

Cayce, Edgar. *Auras*. Virginia Beach, VA: ARE Press, 1973.

Cerminara, Gina. *Many Mansions*. New York: New American Library, 1999.

Davis, Andrew Jackson. *Magic Staff*. Boston: Bela Marsh, 1867.

Dweller, Larry. *Beginner's Guide to Mediumship*. York Beach, ME: Weiser Books, 1997.

Fiore, Dr. Edith. *The Unquiet Dead*. New York: Ballantine Books, 1995.

Garrett, Eileen. *Awareness*. New York: Parapsychology Foundation, 2010.

Guiley, Rosemary. *Harper's Encyclopedia of Mystical and Paranormal Experience*. San Francisco: Harper, 1991.

Guiley, Rosemary Ellen. *Dreamspeak*. New York: Berkeley Books, 2003.

Gunther, John J. *Death Be Not Proud*. New York: Harper Perennial Modern Classics, 2007.

Henry, Ronald, and Kevin Ryerson. *The Future Healer*. New York: iUniverse, 2007.

Hodson, Geoffrey. *The Brotherhood of Angels and Man*. Wheaton, IL: Theosophical Publishing, 1982.

Hutton, Bernard. *Healing Hands*. London: Virgin Books, 1995.

Ireland, Mark. *Messages from the Afterlife*. Berkeley, CA: North Atlantic Books, 2013.

Joslow-Rodewald, Judith, and Patricia West-Barker. *Healing Spirits*. Freedom, CA: Crossing, 2001.

Kirkpatrick, Sidney D., and Nancy Kirkpatrick. *True Tales from the Edgar Cayce Archives*. Virginia Beach, VA: ARE Press, 2016.

Klimo, Jon. *Channeling*. Berkeley CA: North Atlantic Books, 1998.

Leadbeater, C. W. *Clairvoyance*. Amazon Digital Services, 2015.

McMoneagle, Joseph. *The Stargate Chronicles*. New York: Crossroads, 2015.

Merrill, Joseph H. *Healing*. Indianapolis, IN: Summit, 1979.

Myss, Caroline. *Anatomy of the Spirit*. New York: Harmony, 2013.

Newton, Dr. J. R. *The Modern Bethesda*. New York: Newton, 1879.

Olcutt, Henry Steel. *Old Diary Leaves*. Madras, India: C. P. Putnam and Sons, 1895.

Owens, Elizabeth. *Spiritualism and Clairvoyance for Beginners*. Minneapolis: Llewellyn, 2005.

Powell, A. E. *The Astral Body*. Wheaton, IL: Quest, 1927.

Schwartz, Gary. *Afterlife Communication*. Normal, IL: Greater Reality, 2014.

Schultz. Mona Lisa. *All Is Well*. Carlsbad, CA: Hay House, 2014.

Shealy, C. Norman. *Blueprint for Holistic Healing*. Virginia Beach, VA: ARE Press, 2016.

Shumsky, Susan G. *Exploring Auras*. Franklin Lakes, NJ: New Page Books, 2005.

Stearn, Jess. *Yoga Youth and Reincarnation*. Virginia Beach, VA: ARE Press, 1997.

Sugrue, Thomas. *There Is a River*. Virginia Beach, VA: ARE Press, 1997.

Wickland, Dr. Carl. *Thirty Years among the Dead*. Kindle, Locations 15033–15043. Rev. Steven Earl York, Kindle Edition.

Wigmore, Ann. *Why Suffer?* Healthy Living Publications, Kindle Edition, 2013.

Zion, Tina. *Become a Medical Intuitive*. San Francisco: WriteLife, 2015.

INDEX

About the Author

ELAINE KUZMESKUS, director of the New England School of Metaphysics, is a nationally known Spiritualist medium. During more than forty years of mediumship, she has conducted many well-publicized séances, including the 1997 Official Houdini Séance at the Goodspeed Opera House in Haddam, Connecticut. She has been featured on Better Connecticut and the PBS special *Things That Go Bump in the Night* and *The Paranormal View*. Recently, she was a guest on *Coast to Coast* with George Noory. In addition to television and radio appearances, Elaine has conducted events for the Mark Twain Theatre, Lily Dale Assembly, and the Leaning Annex in New York City. She is also the author of five books on mediumship: *Connecticut Ghosts*, *Séance 101: Physical Mediumship*, *The Art of Mediumship*, *The Medium Who Baffled Houdini*, and an autobiography, *The Making of a Medium*.